FAMOUS
DINOSAURS
OF AFRICA

**Anusuya
Chinsamy-Turan**

**Illustrated by
Luis V. Rey**

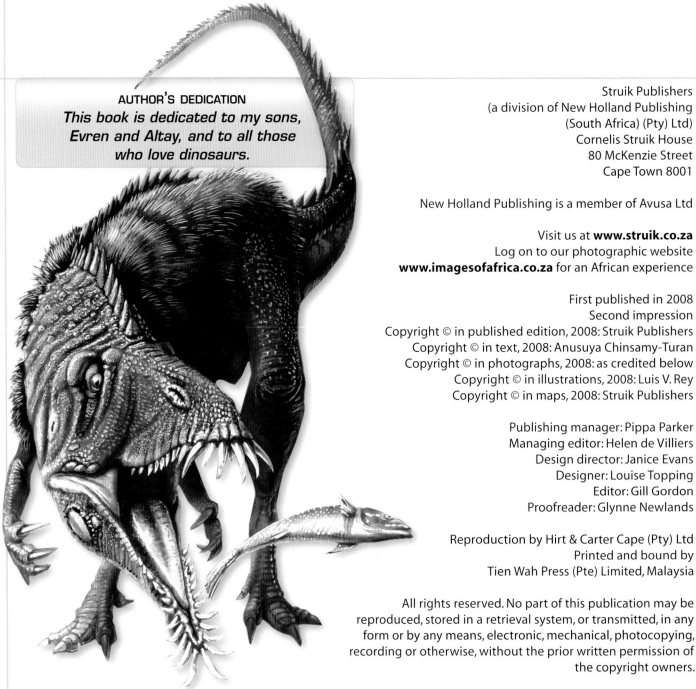

Struik Publishers
(a division of New Holland Publishing
(South Africa) (Pty) Ltd)
Cornelis Struik House
80 McKenzie Street
Cape Town 8001

New Holland Publishing is a member of Avusa Ltd

Visit us at **www.struik.co.za**
Log on to our photographic website
www.imagesofafrica.co.za for an African experience

First published in 2008
Second impression
Copyright © in published edition, 2008: Struik Publishers
Copyright © in text, 2008: Anusuya Chinsamy-Turan
Copyright © in photographs, 2008: as credited below
Copyright © in illustrations, 2008: Luis V. Rey
Copyright © in maps, 2008: Struik Publishers

Publishing manager: Pippa Parker
Managing editor: Helen de Villiers
Design director: Janice Evans
Designer: Louise Topping
Editor: Gill Gordon
Proofreader: Glynne Newlands

Reproduction by Hirt & Carter Cape (Pty) Ltd
Printed and bound by
Tien Wah Press (Pte) Limited, Malaysia

ISBN 978 1 77007 588 7

PHOTO CREDITS:

Key: ACT: Anusuya Chinsamy-Turan; AM: Albany Museum, Grahamstown; BMNH: Berlin Museum of Natural History; BPI: Bernard Price Institute for Palaeontological Research, University of the Witwatersrand; BM: British Museum; IOA: Images of Africa; IVPP: Institute of Vertebrate Palaeontology and Palaeanthropology, China; Iziko: Iziko South African Museum, Cape Town.

Adam Yates/BPI: p20; ACT: pp 4b, 5 (right), 14 (top), 15 (top right, bottom), 30 (bottom left, centre and right), 46 (top left), 51 (top left and right, bottom right), 58 (right), 63 (right); ACT/AM: pp 4d, 50 (bottom left); ACT/BPI: pp 13 (top), 14 (bottom); ACT/IVPP: p4c; ACT/Iziko: pp 4a, 12 (top), 13 (bottom), 16 (bottom), 18 (top left, bottom left, top right, bottom right), 44 (right), 47 (right), 51 (top); Billy de Klerk/AM: pp 50 (bottom right), 51 (left); Billy de Klerk/BM: p 46 (bottom left); BMNH: pp10, 45 (centre and right); Cristiano dal Sasso/Milan Civic Natural History Museum: p 22 (right); David Krause: pp 25 (top and bottom), 60, 61; Evren Turan: p 5 (centre); Hamish Robertson/Iziko: p48; Hein von Horsten/IOA: p5 (left); Jørn Hurum: p 52 (left); Kristi Currey-Rogers: pp 31 (bottom left), 52 (right); Louis Jacobs: pp 32 (top and bottom right), 33 (top and bottom); Lucy Kemp: p63 (top); Luis Chiappe: p 30 (top left); Patti Kane-Vanni: pp 34 (left), 35; Paul Sereno: pp 28, 38, 49 (bottom); Peter Dodson: p9; Philippe Taquet: p54; Robert Reiz/BPI: p12 (bottom); Roger Smith: p17; Samantha van der Riet: p62; Tony Fiorillo/Dallas Museum of Natural History: p32 (left); Willem Hillenius: p58 (left). Author photograph on back cover: SA Woman of the Year. All illustrations by Luis V. Rey except: Anusuya Chinsamy-Turan/Louise Topping: p6; Kristi Currey-Rogers: p31 (bottom left); Samantha van der Riet, pp 7, 8. Louise Topping: poster design and cartography.

Contents

chapter one

Introduction

Dinosaurs roamed our planet for 160 million years and, for much of that time, they were the dominant animals on land. Then, 65 million years ago, an unknown disaster struck Earth and all the dinosaurs died out, except for birds, which are their descendants. The remains of dinosaurs have been discovered on every continent, including Antarctica. This book explores some of the famous dinosaurs discovered in Africa.

Many different sizes and types of dinosaur have been unearthed in Africa, ranging from tiny plant-eating dinosaurs found in Lesotho to the world's largest predatory (meat-eating) dinosaurs, which once prowled across the continent. Some of the bizarre-looking dinosaurs found in Africa include a variety that specialized in eating fish, those with extraordinary adaptations for eating plants, and others with 'sail-like' extensions along their backs. The high concentration of dinosaur bones found in Tendaguru, in Tanzania, makes it a world-famous dinosaur 'graveyard' and gives us a glimpse into the incredible variety of dinosaurs that lived in Africa about 140 million years ago. Many giant long-necked dinosaurs, called sauropods, some measuring up to 25 m in length and weighing several tens of tons, have been unearthed at Tendaguru (see page 40).

Everything we know about dinosaurs comes from their preserved remains, or fossils. Most dinosaurs are known from the fossilized hard parts of their skeletons – their bones and teeth – but, sometimes, fossilized dinosaur eggs (some with tiny skeletons inside them), dinosaur nests, or tracks (footprints), are also discovered. It is from all this evidence that scientists can uncover important clues about the lives and times of these spectacular creatures.

Dinosaur fossils come in many forms and from many parts of the world, as depicted in the photographs below:

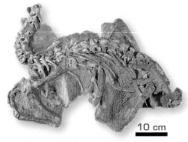

10 cm

Skeleton of *Heterodontosaurus*, a South African dinosaur.

Dinosaur tracks in Argentina.

A nest of dinosaur eggs from China.

1 cm

Sauropod teeth from South Africa.

Theropod dinosaurs (see page 6) include the fish-eating *Masiakasaurus*, (left, see page 25) and predatory *Syntarsus* (right, see page 56); both were bipedal, meaning they walked on two legs.

Although the word 'dinosaur' means 'terrible lizard', dinosaurs were not lizards! They were specialized reptiles that descended from a prehistoric group of reptiles called archosaurs (ARK-oh-SAWR), which means 'ruling reptiles'. In addition to being the ancestors of dinosaurs, the archosaurs also gave rise to flying reptiles, called pterosaurs (TARE-uh-SAWR) and crocodilians, whose later descendants, crocodiles and birds, are the only members of this group to survive into modern times (see the dinosaur family tree on page 6).

Dinosaurs had many unique features that set them apart from other reptiles. For example, they had an 'erect' or upright posture (like birds and mammals) with their legs positioned directly beneath their bodies, helping to support their body weight. This is in contrast to the 'sprawling' posture of most lizards, whose legs stick out from their sides, with their body hanging between their limbs. Crocodiles and alligators have a semi-erect posture, which is in-between that of a fully erect posture and a sprawling posture.

Upright posture

Sprawling posture

Semi-erect posture

Saurischians and ornithischians:
All dinosaurs can be divided into two groups – saurischians or ornithischians – depending on the shape and arrangement of their hip bones: the **ilium** (which attaches to the spinal column), the **ischium** and the **pubis**.

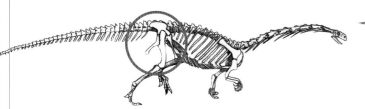 

The saurischians (soar-ISH-ee-un), or 'lizard-hipped' dinosaurs, have a three-pronged hip bone, with the pubis facing forwards.

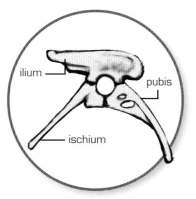

In the ornithischians (ORE-nih-THISH-ee-un), or 'bird-hipped' dinosaurs, the pubis extends backwards.

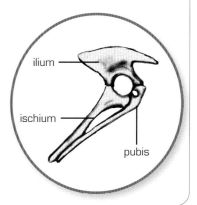

THE DINOSAUR FAMILY TREE

The archosaurs are the common ancestors of pterosaurs (TARE-uh-SAWR), crocodilians and dinosaurs. Dinosaurs are separated into ornithischians (ORE-nih-THISH-ee-un) and saurischians (soar-ISH-ee-un) on the basis of the hip structure, as described on page 5. All the ornithischians were plant-eaters (herbivores), while the saurischians were both meat-eaters (carnivores) and plant eaters. The most famous of the plant-eaters are the sauropods, or long-necked dinosaurs (see page 40). The meat-eaters are known as the theropods. These bipedal (walking on two legs) carnivores diversified into a range of different sizes and shapes, including small forms, like *Nqwebasaurus* (see page 50), as well as gigantic predatory forms, like *Carcharodontosaurus* (see page 28).

Birds, which are closely related to theropods, are the only descendants of dinosaurs that survived the mass extinction event that took place at the end of the Cretaceous period, some 65 million years ago (see geological timeline below).

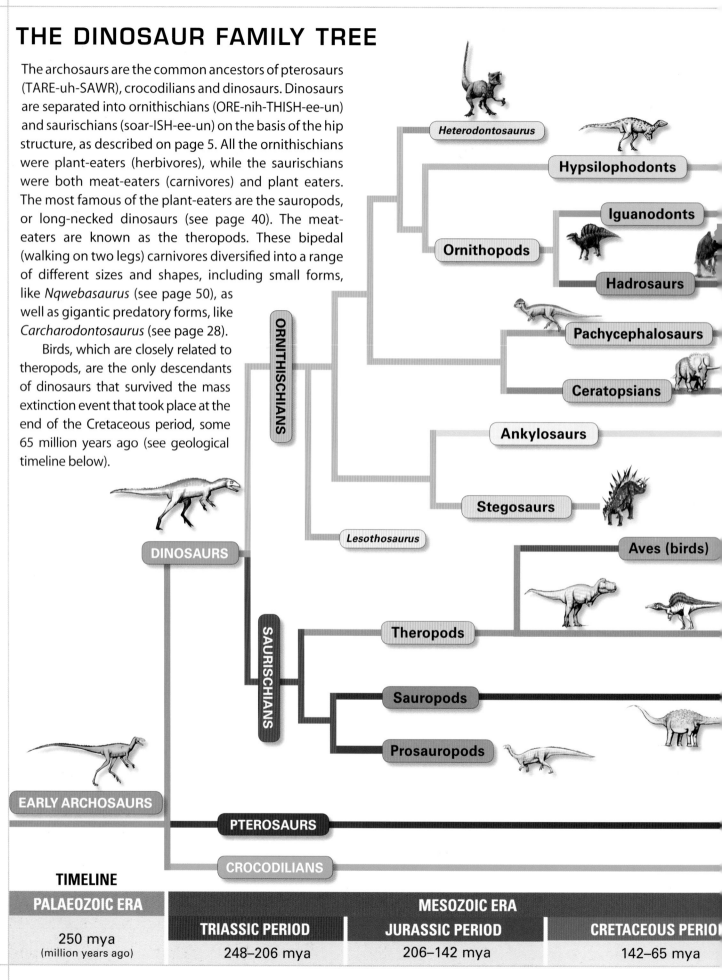

Heterodontosaurus

Hypsilophodonts

Iguanodonts

Ornithopods

Hadrosaurs

Pachycephalosaurs

Ceratopsians

Ankylosaurs

ORNITHISCHIANS

Stegosaurs

Lesothosaurus

Aves (birds)

DINOSAURS

Theropods

SAURISCHIANS

Sauropods

Prosauropods

EARLY ARCHOSAURS

PTEROSAURS

CROCODILIANS

TIMELINE

PALAEOZOIC ERA	MESOZOIC ERA		
250 mya (million years ago)	**TRIASSIC PERIOD** 248–206 mya	**JURASSIC PERIOD** 206–142 mya	**CRETACEOUS PERIO** 142–65 mya

CONTINENTAL MOVEMENT

The outer crust of Earth is made up of rock plates on which the continents are located. During Earth's long history, these plates have moved, changing the surface of the planet and affecting the movement and, hence, the distribution and radiation (spread) of dinosaurs and other animals.

MESOZOIC ERA

TRIASSIC PERIOD 248–206 mya

The earliest dinosaurs evolved during the Triassic period, when all the continents were joined into a single landmass, called Pangaea. Many different reptiles existed at this time, including the pterosaurs, or flying reptiles. There is also evidence that small mammals were in existence during this period.

JURASSIC PERIOD 206–142 mya

In the Jurassic period, the continents separated into a northern landmass, called Laurasia, and a southern landmass, Gondwana, which consisted of what we now call Africa, Madagascar, India, Australia, South America and Antarctica. By now, there were many different dinosaurs and, towards the end of the Jurassic period, birds evolved from the theropods.

CRETACEOUS PERIOD 142–65 mya

During the Cretaceous period, both Laurasia and Gondwana split into smaller landmasses and these eventually formed the continents that we know today.

EXTINCTION OF DINOSAURS

Dinosaurs lived on Earth for 160 million years, but no dinosaur fossils are found in rocks that are younger than 65 million years old. No-one knows why dinosaurs became extinct. Many scientists believe that a global catastrophe was caused by a combination of several events: an asteroid colliding with Earth, a series of volcanic outpourings and dramatic sea-level changes. All these events are known to have happened at the end of the Cretaceous period (see Timeline opposite), and may have led to the collapse of the reign of dinosaurs.

By the time our ancestors arrived on the scene , dinosaurs had been extinct for more than 62 million years. So, contrary to the popular American cartoon, 'The Flintstones', humans and dinosaurs never lived at the same time!

CENOZOIC ERA

65 mya →

HOW DID A DINOSAUR BECOME A FOSSIL?

Only a small percentage of all dinosaurs that lived on Earth are preserved as fossils. This is because fossils form only in certain circumstances, when a number of particular events occur in a particular sequence, as depicted below.

1

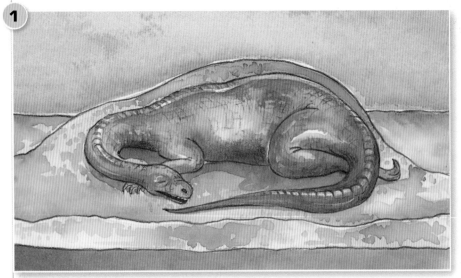

Soon after they died, some dinosaurs' bodies were covered by a layer of sand or mud (sediment), perhaps from a downpour or flood; this reduced the chance of the remains being eaten by predators or scavengers, and protected them from being scattered or damaged. The soft tissues (skin, muscles, blood, nerves, etc.) would soon begin to decompose, and eventually only the bony skeletons would remain.

2

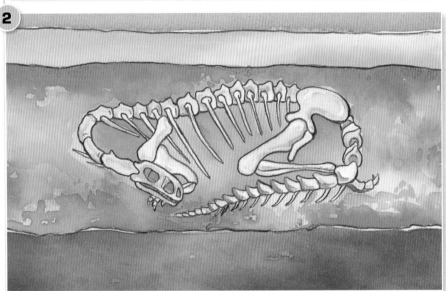

Over time, more and more layers of sediment would cover the bones so that the remains became buried deep under the surface. Eventually, the sediment would become compressed to form the rocks in which the animals' bones and teeth are preserved.

3

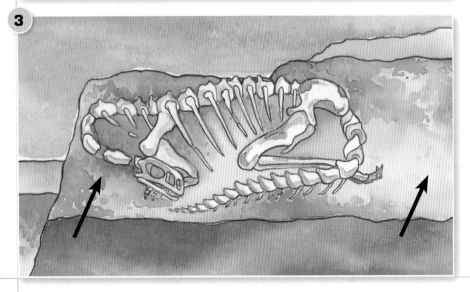

Fossils can lie entombed for millions of years, until the overlying rocks weather away or the rock strata are uplifted (see arrows) as a result of geological processes. Eventually bones may be exposed on the surface, hinting at what may lie buried in the rock. Fossil bones are often discovered during mining operations and road construction or when digging foundations for new buildings.

EXCAVATING FOSSIL BONES

When fossilized bones are discovered, a **palaeontologist** is usually contracted to excavate the fossil from the ground. The pictures below show scientist David Krause (see picture 1) and his team excavating the remains of 70-million-year-old dinosaurs discovered in northern Madagascar.

Palaeontologists are scientists who dig up and study fossils to learn more about extinct animals and plants, and when and why they died.

1

Often only a small part of a fossilized bone is visible on the surface and the palaeontologist has to remove the surrounding rock with great care. Once he (or she) is certain that all the bone on the surface is exposed, he then needs to work out the depth to which the bones extend into the underlying rock.

2

The palaeontologist carefully works around the surface of the exposed bone to create a mushroom-like structure with the fossil on top of a base of rock.

3

The exposed surface is covered with strips of cloth and plaster of Paris. Once the plaster hardens to form a 'jacket' to protect the fossil, the stem of the 'mushroom' is cut and the fossil and its surrounding rock are turned over and jacketed on the other side (the 'stem' part).

4

When the entire block of dinosaur bone, together with its surrounding rock, is encased in plaster of Paris, it can be safely transported to a museum or university for further preparation and study.

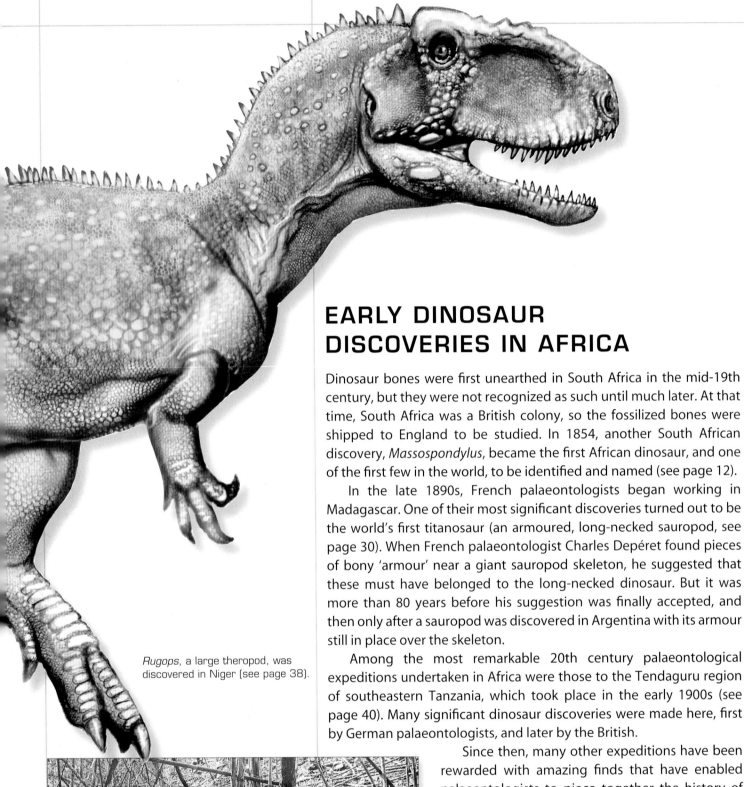

Rugops, a large theropod, was discovered in Niger (see page 38).

EARLY DINOSAUR DISCOVERIES IN AFRICA

Dinosaur bones were first unearthed in South Africa in the mid-19th century, but they were not recognized as such until much later. At that time, South Africa was a British colony, so the fossilized bones were shipped to England to be studied. In 1854, another South African discovery, *Massospondylus*, became the first African dinosaur, and one of the first few in the world, to be identified and named (see page 12).

In the late 1890s, French palaeontologists began working in Madagascar. One of their most significant discoveries turned out to be the world's first titanosaur (an armoured, long-necked sauropod, see page 30). When French palaeontologist Charles Depéret found pieces of bony 'armour' near a giant sauropod skeleton, he suggested that these must have belonged to the long-necked dinosaur. But it was more than 80 years before his suggestion was finally accepted, and then only after a sauropod was discovered in Argentina with its armour still in place over the skeleton.

Among the most remarkable 20th century palaeontological expeditions undertaken in Africa were those to the Tendaguru region of southeastern Tanzania, which took place in the early 1900s (see page 40). Many significant dinosaur discoveries were made here, first by German palaeontologists, and later by the British.

Since then, many other expeditions have been rewarded with amazing finds that have enabled palaeontologists to piece together the history of dinosaurs in Africa, as well as their relationships to dinosaurs found on other continents. This book cannot include every African dinosaur discovered, but it highlights some of the most famous and remarkable dinosaurs that roamed across Africa millions of years ago.

German palaeontologist Werner Janensch (right), and local helper Salim Tombali, with a number of large dinosaur bones discovered at the Tendaguru site.

THE FIRST DINOSAUR

Over the years, the fossilized remains of many different types of dinosaur have been found in various locations around the world. The earliest-known dinosaur, called *Eoraptor*, which means 'Dawn Thief', was found in Argentina, in rocks that are about 230 million years old. It is estimated that, over a period of about 155 million years, dinosaurs spread across the planet to become the dominant land animals (see Timeline on page 6).

Some dinosaurs, including *Eoraptor*, were small, weighing only a few kilograms, but others, such as *Argentinosaurus* (ARE-jen-TEEN-oh-SAW-rus), the heaviest dinosaur ever known, weighed over 100 tons (about 18 times the weight of an African bull elephant).

About 230 million years ago, mammals were small rodent-like animals; many of them probably fell victim to *Eoraptor*, the earliest predatory dinosaur.

chapter two

The first to be named

ZIMBABWE

SOUTH AFRICA — LESOTHO

Although *Massospondylus* was not the first dinosaur discovered in Africa, it has the distinction of being one of the earliest dinosaurs in the world – and the first African one – to be formally described and named. In 1853, 55 fragments of fossil bone were unearthed in the Harrismith area of the Drakensberg. The bones were shipped off to England and ended up at the Royal College of Surgeons, where they were studied by palaeontologist Sir Richard Owen, who is famous for naming dinosaurs 'terrible lizards'. In 1854, he briefly described the assortment of bones and named this southern African dinosaur '*Massospondylus*'.

FACTS

Name: *Massospondylus*
(MASS-oh-SPON-DIE-lus)
Meaning: 'Longer vertebrae'
Classification: Prosauropod
Size: 5 m long
Weight: 250 kg
Diet: Plants
Found: South Africa, Lesotho, Zimbabwe
When: Early Jurassic, 190 million years ago

MASSOSPONDYLUS

Massospondylus (MASS-oh-SPON-DIE-lus) was a medium-sized plant-eating dinosaur that was fairly common in southern Africa. It is known from numerous specimens collected from a number of Early Jurassic locations in southern Africa.

Many different-sized individuals, from tiny embryos still inside eggs to juveniles, teenagers and adults, have been recovered from the famous 'red beds' of the Karoo basin (see page 17), making *Massospondylus* the best-represented African dinosaur, and one of the most thoroughly studied of all dinosaurs.

up close

Massospondylus' teeth were about 1 cm long, leaf-shaped, or oval, with coarsely serrated edges (left). Although their teeth were not adapted for grinding plant matter, they may have been able to eat tough plants that would have been shredded (cut-up) by their serrated teeth.

Several specimens of *Massospondylus* have been found with gastroliths ('stomach stones') in the stomach area. The stones probably helped them to digest tough plant material (see pages 51 and 63).

When Canadian palaeontologist Robert Reiz studied some *Massospondylus* embryos (right) discovered in the Karoo (see page 14), he noticed that the embryos had some striking features. These included unusually large eye sockets, and forelimbs and hind limbs that were equal in length. This is different from the arrangement of the limbs in the adults, whose forelimbs were much shorter. Reiz suggested that perhaps the babies walked on all four limbs when they hatched, but that the length of their limbs changed as they matured and, as adults, they walked on their hind limbs. We can't be certain at what age this change in limb proportions occurred. This fossil is in the collection of the Bernard Price Institute (Palaeontology) at the University of the Witwatersrand.

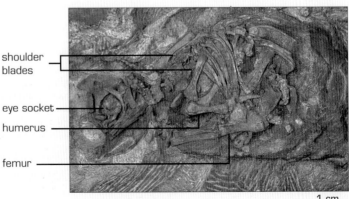

shoulder blades

eye socket

humerus

femur

1 cm

The *Massospondylus* on the right is in a quadrupedal stance (standing on all four legs), while the one on the left rears up on its hind limbs. Notice the size difference between its back and front legs.

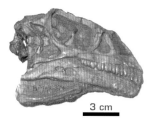

3 cm

The fossilized skull of a juvenile *Massospondylus*; the scale bar gives an idea of how small it is.

Does a herbivore need claws?

Massospondylus' hand had five fingers (digits). The fifth and fourth digits were small and poorly developed, but the first finger, or thumb, ended in a large, curved claw. *Massospondylus* is thought to have been herbivorous (plant-eating), so it is surprising that it had such a vicious-looking claw. Some scientists think the large claw indicates that *Massospondylus* was not a strict vegetarian, and may have been an omnivore (an animal that eats both plant matter and meat).

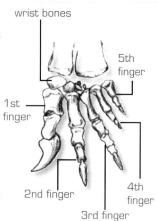

wrist bones

5th finger

1st finger

2nd finger

3rd finger

4th finger

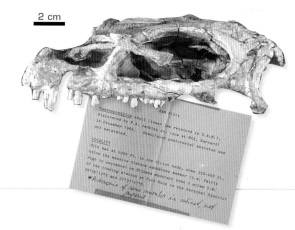

2 cm

Side view of an adult *Massospondylus* skull found in 1966, along with its original museum identification catalogue card. The card provides information about the discoverer and where exactly the skull was found. In the past, this information would be handwritten into a book called a collections catalogue. Nowadays the data is entered into a computerized database. This skull is part of the Earth Sciences Karoo collections at the Iziko South African Museum in Cape Town.

UNSOLVED

• *Massospondylus* had shorter forelimbs (front legs) than hind limbs (back legs), and this has led to considerable debate among scientists about whether it was bipedal (walked on its hind limbs) or quadrupedal (walked on all four limbs). It is possible that it was quadrupedal, but could rear up on its hind limbs, as depicted in the illustration above.

• Since the tiny embryos lacked teeth, and had big heads and poorly developed pelvic girdles, researchers have suggested that *Massospondylus* babies were not independent when they hatched and needed their parents to provide food and care for them, but this cannot be proven.

In 1978, Professor James Kitching, who is world-famous for having collected tons of fossil bones of a variety of extinct southern African animals, discovered several fossilized eggs in a road cutting called 'Rooidraai' in the Golden Gate Highlands National Park, near Clarens in the Free State.

The eggs were about 6 cm in size and more or less round. Tiny, delicate bone fragments of embryos were clearly visible on the surface of some of the 'broken' eggs. At the time, Kitching recognized that they were dinosaur eggs, and he suggested that they might be *Massospondylus* eggs, since it seems to have been the most common dinosaur in the area.

In 2005, six of the eggs were carefully prepared for study by removing the rock surrounding the eggs. This long, intricate process took about a year to finish. On completion, tiny fossilized embryos were revealed inside the eggs (see below and page 12). Two of the embryos were further examined and they showed quite clearly that the eggs were indeed those of *Massospondylus*.

A number of fossilized dinosaur eggs were discovered by James Kitching at the Rooidraai site in the Free State (left). Two tiny embryos can clearly be seen among the eggs, which measure approximately 6 cm in length (below left; see page 12 for detail). In addition to the fossilized dinosaur eggs, two partial skeletons of adult *Massospondylus* were also exposed in this locality, and several other dinosaur skeletons occured within 500 m of the site. These eggs are in the collection of the Bernard Price Institute (Palaeontology) at the University of the Witwatersrand.

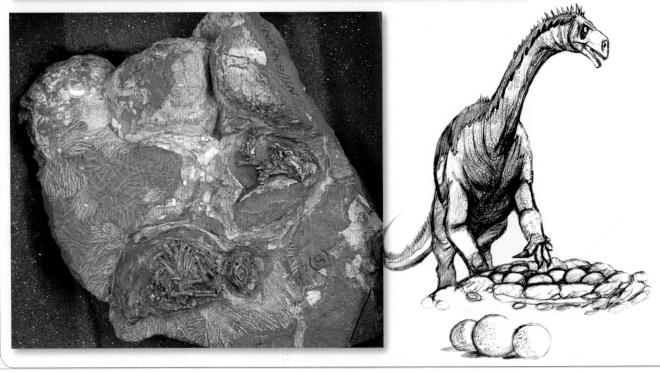

WHAT CAN DINOSAUR BONES TELL US?

Studies of fossilized dinosaur bones provide a great deal of information about these prehistoric creatures. Just by looking at an individual specimen's bones, we can establish its overall size and shape, and how its different bones worked together and the kind of movements they allowed. However, if a thin section of a bone (about half the thickness of a strand of human hair) is put under a microscope, it will reveal details that are not visible just by looking at the whole bone.

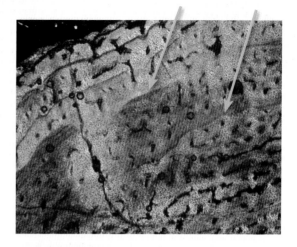

Even after millions of years of fossilization, the microscopic structure contained within dinosaur bones is still preserved. Studying bone sections allows us to find out details about the animal's biology, such as how old an individual dinosaur is, and whether its growth was affected by seasonal conditions.

Three African dinosaurs are well-represented by different-sized individuals (from young juveniles to teenagers and adults): *Massospondylus* and *Syntarsus* (from southern Africa, see pages 12 and 56) and *Dryosaurus* (DRY-oh-SAW-rus), an ornithischian dinosaur recovered from the Tendaguru region in Tanzania. By examining the microstructure of these dinosaurs, Anusuya Chinsamy-Turan was able to deduce information about their growth dynamics and overall biology.

Sections of a dinosaur bone showing several growth rings caused by periods of alternating fast and slow growth. Arrows indicate periods of slower growth.

Massospondylus and *Syntarsus* have a bone microstructure that shows a cyclical growth pattern, with alternating periods of fast and slow growth, which resulted in the formation of 'growth rings' (similar to tree rings) in their bones. This pattern of growth is similar to the type of bone formed in reptiles. Studies of modern reptiles have shown that the wider rings mark periods of fast growth, while narrow bands reflect slower growth (sometimes even periods of no growth), and that one period of fast growth and one of slowed growth are formed annually. Thus, by counting the number of rings in a bone, you can obtain an estimate of the age of an individual; this study is termed skeletochronology. By applying skeletochronology to the bones of *Massospondylus* and *Syntarsus*, Chinsamy-Turan was able to develop growth curves for these dinosaurs, and determine that *Massospondylus* took 15 years to grow from a tiny hatchling to an adult, while the much smaller meat-eater, *Syntarsus*, took eight years to reach adult size.

The internal bone structure of *Dryosaurus* showed that it did not form growth rings in its bones, and did not have a cyclical growth pattern like that of the southern African dinosaurs. Instead, the study of *Dryosaurus* bones revealed that they grew very rapidly as juveniles, although their growth slowed down later on.

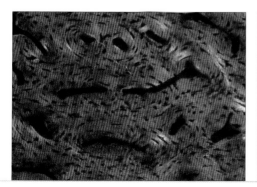

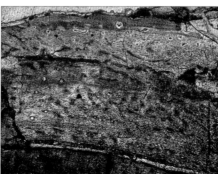

FAR LEFT: High magnification image of *Syntarsus* bone showing the bone microstructure. The small dark spots indicate where bone cells once lived, while the larger dark areas are where blood vessels occurred.
LEFT: A thin section of *Syntarsus* bone; the growth rings in the bone are clearly visible.

chapter three

The oldest African dinosaurs

SOUTH AFRICA ——→ ←—— LESOTHO

Some of the earliest ornithischian and sauropod dinosaurs ever discovered come from Africa. Two dinosaurs from the Early Jurassic period – *Heterodontosaurus* from South Africa and *Lesothosaurus* from the mountain kingdom of Lesotho – are the best-represented early ornithischian (bird-hipped) dinosaurs that show special adaptations for eating plants (herbivory). *Antetonitris*, from the Late Triassic, is considered to be the world's earliest known sauropod (long-necked dinosaur).

FACTS

Name: *Lesothosaurus*
(leh-SOO-too-SAW-rus)
Meaning: 'Lizard from Lesotho'
Classification: Ornithischian
Size: 1 m
Weight: 9 kg
Diet: Plants
Found: Lesotho
When: Early Jurassic,
208–200 million years ago

LESOTHOSAURUS

Lesothosaurus (leh-SOO-too-SAW-rus) was a small, lightly built, long-tailed, plant-eating dinosaur that walked on its hind legs (i.e. it was bipedal). The long, slender back legs suggest that it was a fast runner. It had a long, flexible neck, a short skull with large eye sockets, and a short snout.

Short, pointy teeth were located at the tip of the upper jaw, but the lower jaws seem to have ended in bone that was probably covered with keratin (the same material that makes up the beaks of birds, and fingernails in humans). This beak-like structure at the tip of its jaws may have been very effective in nipping off small pieces of plant shoots or foliage. The teeth were oval and could have been used for cutting up food, but not for shredding plants. The long tail probably helped it to balance when it ran.

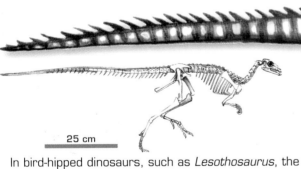

25 cm

In bird-hipped dinosaurs, such as *Lesothosaurus*, the pubic bone extends backwards (see also page 5).

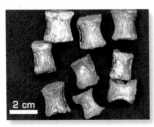

2 cm

1 cm

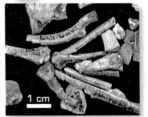

1 cm

1 cm

Bones recovered from a fossil of *Lesothosaurus* include (from left to right) vertebrae; tooth, showing fine serrations on its leaf-like edges; ribs and other bone fragments, and two toes (metatarsals).

DISCOVERING DINOSAURS

Finding dinosaur bones is not difficult, but you have to know what you are doing! First, you need to be sure that the rocks you are looking at are the 'right' age. To do this, you need a geological map, which shows the different ages of rocks. You should concentrate your search on rocks dating from the Late Triassic to Cretaceous periods, since this is when dinosaurs were around (see page 7). In the Karoo basin, dinosaurs are found in rocks dating to the Late Triassic to Early Jurassic (see page 14), while Cretaceous-age rocks are located in the Algoa Basin in the Eastern Cape (see pages 46 and 50).

Once you find exposed rocks of the right age, you'll need to keep your eyes firmly on the ground to spot any fossil bones that may be weathering out of the rock. If you see something that could be a dinosaur bone, you will need to contact a palaeontologist to excavate the bones. In South Africa, it is illegal to collect fossil bones. (Why? Well, imagine if you discovered a rare fossil and kept it at home; the scientific community would know nothing about it and would not be able to study it to uncover its secrets, or share the findings with other scientists!)

Dinosaurs found in the Karoo basin are usually recovered from a rock formation called the Elliot Formation. This formation is commonly known as the 'red beds' because of the characteristic red colour of the rocks. The colour comes from a high concentration of iron oxides (mainly haematite) in the rock, and one of the distinctive features of the fossils found in this area is that the bones are often surrounded by a 'crust' of haematite.

In the eastern Free State, the 'red beds' of the Elliot Formation are overlaid by the huge sandstone cliffs of the Clarens Formation.

The rocks of the Elliot and Clarens formations have distinctive colours and features; the lump in the foreground is a vertebra of a prosauropod dinosaur (it is encrusted with haematite).

Local palaeontologist Roger Smith excavates a *Massospondylus* femur (thigh bone). Notice the reddish colour of the bone.

HETERODONTOSAURUS

FACTS

Name: *Heterodontosaurus*
  (HET-ur-oh-DON-toe-SAW-rus)
Meaning: 'Different-toothed
  lizard'
Classification: Ornithopod
Size: 1 m long
Weight: 9 kg
Diet: Plants
Found: South Africa
When: Early Jurassic,
  208–200 million years ago

Heterodontosaurus (HET-ur-oh-DON-toe-SAW-rus) is a plant-eating dinosaur from the Early Jurassic 'red beds' of the Karoo basin (see page 17).

In its jaw structure, *Heterodontosaurus* shows remarkable adaptations for eating plants. As its name, 'different-toothed lizard', suggests, it had at least three different types of teeth in its jaws, including tusk-like canines at the sides of the mouth (see 'Up close' panel below left). The joint between the upper and lower jaws rotated to allow a scissor-like cutting action between the cheek teeth. The grinding surfaces on the teeth suggest that it had a sophisticated chewing mechanism, which included side-to-side grinding.

Like *Lesothosaurus*, the 'beak' at the front of its mouth was probably covered by a tough keratin-like material, which allowed it to crush and grind plant material. *Heterodontosaurus* also had specially developed cheek pouches at the sides of its mouth which helped it to hold food in its mouth.

up close

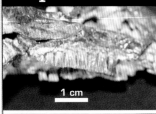

1 cm

1 cm

These pictures show *Heterodontosaurus'* postcanine teeth (those at the sides of its jaw, behind the canine teeth). The top picture shows the side view, while the bottom picture shows a view from beneath the skull, with the flat, crushing surface of the teeth clearly visible.

UNSOLVED

Why would a herbivore have such long canine teeth?
Scientists think the long, sharp canine teeth may have played a role in asserting dominance or for mate recognition, or perhaps even for some unknown aspect of its feeding behaviour. In the illustration (below left), you can see how the tip of the canines in the lower jaw fit into a notch in the upper jaw. The drawing is based on the actual fossil skull (below right), which clearly shows the gap in the upper jaw into which the canines fitted.

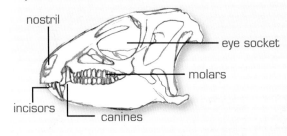

nostril — eye socket — molars — incisors — canines

notch in upper jaw   2 cm

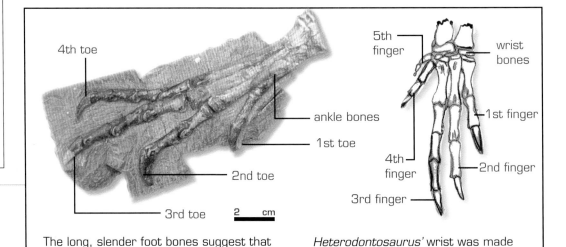

4th toe — 5th finger — wrist bones — ankle bones — 1st toe — 1st finger — 2nd toe — 4th finger — 2nd finger — 3rd toe — 2 cm — 3rd finger

The long, slender foot bones suggest that *Heterodontosaurus* was a fast runner.

Heterodontosaurus' wrist was made up of several bones, which suggests that it was quite flexible. It had long slender fingers, each ending in a claw.

10 cm

OPPOSITE: Although *Heterodontosaurus* was a herbivore, its pointy canines may have made it appear more vicious, and may have been used to threaten or ward off predators.

ANTETONITRUS

FACTS

Name: *Antetonitrus*
  (An-TEE-ton-EYE-trus)
Meaning: 'Before thunder'
Classification: Sauropod
Size: 8–10 m long,
  hip height 1.5–2 m
Diet: Plants
Found: South Africa
When: Late Triassic,
  221–210 million years ago

Antetonitrus (An-TEE-ton-EYE-trus) is famous for being the first of the long-necked dinosaurs (sauropods), which were some of the largest animals ever to have lived on land. However, the earliest members of this group did not start off very big. *Antetonitrus* is estimated to have been about 8–10 m long – only one third of the size of some of the giant sauropods of the Mesozoic period (see page 6).

When South African palaeontologist, James Kitching, discovered *Antetonitrus* in the Free State more than 25 years ago, it was thought to be a prosauropod dinosaur. However, when the skeletal remains were recently re-examined by palaeontologist Adam Yates, they were found to have characteristics that were more like those of the sauropods. In 2003, Yates named the dinosaur *Antetonitrus* and today it is recognized as the earliest known sauropod. The name means 'before thunder' and refers to the fact that it lived before *Brontosaurus*, the 'thunder lizard'. (*Brontosaurus* is now known as *Apatosaurus*.)

The *Antetonitrus* fossil find comprises parts of a disjointed skeleton, with several vertebrae (back bones), parts of both front limbs and part of the left hind limb (see below). Although the bones were separate when they were found, they were near enough to each other to suggest they were from one individual. The bones of the vertebrae were unfused, which indicates it was probably a young dinosaur that was still growing when it died and had not yet reached its adult size.

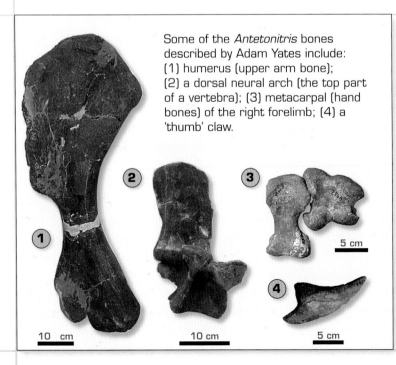

Some of the *Antetonitris* bones described by Adam Yates include:
(1) humerus (upper arm bone);
(2) a dorsal neural arch (the top part of a vertebra); (3) metacarpal (hand bones) of the right forelimb; (4) a 'thumb' claw.

5 cm

10 cm   10 cm   5 cm

chapter four

The fish-eating dinosaurs

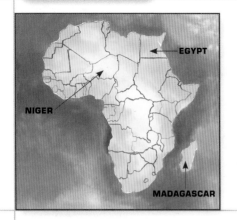

The fish-eating dinosaurs, or Spinosaurids, are specialized theropod (meat-eating) dinosaurs. They are characterized by having long, narrow, crocodile-like snouts that are packed with pointy, conical teeth. Not many fish-eating dinosaurs are known but, in Africa, three dinosaurs show unusual adaptations for a diet specializing in fish: *Spinosaurus* from Egypt, *Suchomimus* from Niger and *Masiakasaurus* from Madagascar.

FACTS

Name: *Spinosaurus*
(SPY-no-SAW-rus)
Meaning: 'Spined lizard'
Classification: Theropod
Size: 12–17 m long
Weight: 3.6–9 tons
Diet: Fish
Found: Egypt
When: Mid-Cretaceous,
95 million years ago

SPINOSAURUS

In 1912, the remains of a bizarre-looking dinosaur, with unusually shaped vertebrae (backbones) and a peculiar lower jaw with crocodile-like teeth, was discovered in the Baharîya oasis in central Egypt. The fossilized bones were shipped to Germany in 1915, but the material was destroyed in 1944 by the Allied bombing of Munich. Fortunately, a Bavarian palaeontologist, Ernst Stromer, had already studied the fossilized remains, and his detailed descriptions and illustrations survived. Stromer named this rather unusual dinosaur, *Spinosaurus aegypticus*, the 'spined lizard from Egypt'.

Spinosaurus (SPY-no-SAW-rus) had a long, narrow skull with a large number of teeth, and huge claws on its hands, which possibly helped it to catch fish. One of the most unusual features of this dinosaur was the 'sail' along its back that was formed by a number of 1.7-metre-long bony extensions of its backbone.

up close

Spinosaurus had a long, narrow skull with many sharp teeth, which possibly helped it to catch and hold wet, slippery fish (see illustration opposite).

UNSOLVED

It is uncertain what function *Spinosaurus'* 'sail' served, but it is possible that it helped to maintain the animal's body temperature.

A partial skull of *Spinosaurus* on display in the Civic Natural History Museum in Milan, Italy. Palaeontologist Cristiano dal Sasso (right) and his colleagues have determined that this almost metre-long snout belonged to an animal they estimate at about 17 m in length. If their estimate is correct, *Spinosaurus* would have been one of the biggest predatory dinosaurs known.

Spinosaurus' sail was formed by bony extensions that ran along its backbone.

2 m

The shaded part of the snout (above) represents the fossil part on display in Milan.

SUCHOMIMUS

FACTS

Name: *Suchomimus tenerensis*
(SOOK-o-MIME-us)
Meaning: 'Crocodile mimic'
Classification: Theropod
Size: 11 m long; 3.6 m tall
Weight: 5 tons
Diet: Fish
Found: Ténéré Desert, Niger
When: Mid-Cretaceous,
110–100 million years ago

In 1997, University of Chicago palaeontologist, Paul Sereno, and his team discovered one of the most complete fossils of a fish-eating dinosaur in the Ténéré Desert, Niger, and called it *Suchomimus*, which means 'crocodile mimic'. Like *Spinosaurus*, this dinosaur also had a sail on its back, formed by blade-like extensions from its backbone. The skull was extremely well preserved and clearly showed that its snout was rather long, flattish and narrow. Together, the long snout and huge claws (the thumb-claw measures 33 cm) would have made *Suchomimus* very effective at catching fish.

Suchomimus had a long, flat, narrow skull, robust forelimbs with huge claws, and blade-like vertebral spines that formed a low sail over its back.

Suchomimus being attacked by *Sarchosuchus*, the giant 12-metre-long crocodile that lived at the same time.

MASIAKASAURUS

The most recently discovered fish-eating dinosaur, *Masiakasaurus* (Mah-SHEE-kah-SAW-rus), was excavated in 2001 in Madagascar by an American and Malagasy team led by palaeontologists Scott Sampson, from the University of Utah, and David Krause, from the University of New York at Stony Brook (see page 9).

Unlike *Spinosaurus* and *Suchomimus*, *Masiakasaurus* was small, only about the size of an adult German shepherd dog. One of its most distinctive features was the teeth at the front of its lower jaw. These were cone-shaped with hooked tips, and protruded outwards almost horizontally from the jaw. Only after the fourth tooth did the teeth take on a more normal (vertical) arrangement and start to look like the teeth of other meat-eating dinosaurs. This unusual arrangement and type of teeth suggests that *Masiakasaurus* may have been a fish-eating dinosaur, although it probably also ate other prey items.

Masiakasaurus' species name is *Knopfleri* (nawp-FLAIR-ee); it was named after Mark Knopfler, singer-guitarist of Dire Straits, whose music the palaeontologists listened to while looking for dinosaurs in Madagascar.

FACTS

Name: *Masiakasaurus*
(Mah-SHEE-kah-SAW-rus)
Meaning: 'Vicious lizard'
Classification: Theropod
Size: 2 m long
Weight: 35 kg
Diet: Fish and meat
Found: Madagascar
When: Late Cretaceous,
70–65 million years ago

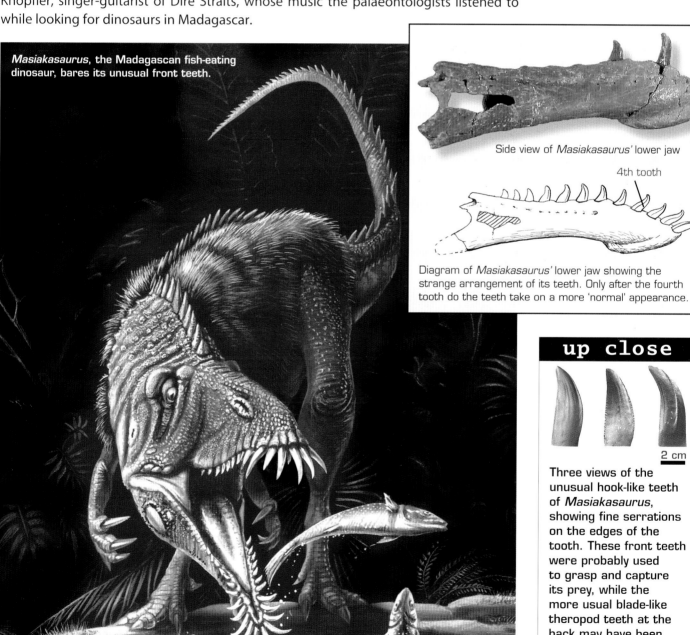

Masiakasaurus, the Madagascan fish-eating dinosaur, bares its unusual front teeth.

Side view of *Masiakasaurus'* lower jaw

4th tooth

Diagram of *Masiakasaurus'* lower jaw showing the strange arrangement of its teeth. Only after the fourth tooth do the teeth take on a more 'normal' appearance.

up close

2 cm

Three views of the unusual hook-like teeth of *Masiakasaurus*, showing fine serrations on the edges of the tooth. These front teeth were probably used to grasp and capture its prey, while the more usual blade-like theropod teeth at the back may have been used for cutting and slicing its victims.

BARYONYX AND OTHER FISH-EATING DINOSAURS

Predatory fish-eating dinosaurs have been discovered in other parts of the world, notably in Europe and Brazil. Two Brazilian forms, *Irritator* (EAR-ih-TATE-or) and *Angaturama* (ANGH-uh-tuh-RAH-ma), are known from partial skull remains, while the older European *Baryonyx* (BAR-ee-ON-icks) is one of the most complete dinosaurs ever recovered from England.

Evidence of *Baryonyx'* fish-eating lifestyle was confirmed by the presence within its body cavity of fish scales, which appeared to be acid-etched by stomach juices. Interestingly, the remains of a young *Iguanodon* (an early plant-eating dinosaur) were also found within the body cavity – clearly indicating that fish was not the only item on this theropod's dinner menu.

FACTS

Name: *Baryonyx*
(BAR-ee-ON-icks)
Meaning: 'Heavy claw' – after the large claw on its thumb
Classification: Theropod
Size: 9 m long
Weight: 1 500 kg
Diet: Fish and meat
Found: Southern England
When: Early Cretaceous, 125 million years ago

UNSOLVED

The relationship between the fish-eating dinosaurs from Africa, Brazil and Europe is quite complicated. One would think that *Spinosaurus* and *Suchomimus* would be closely related, since they were both found in North Africa but, according to American palaeontologist Paul Sereno, *Suchomimus* is more closely related to the European *Baryonyx*. This finding is important for helping us to understand how and when these dinosaurs evolved on different continents.

The spinosaurid *Baryonyx* (above and left), discovered in England in 1983, is closely related to the African spinosaurid, *Suchomimus*.

chapter five

The biggest meat-eating dinosaur of all time

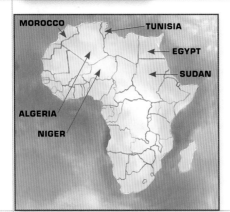

MOROCCO TUNISIA EGYPT SUDAN ALGERIA NIGER

Carcharodontosaurus was an enormous predatory meat-eating dinosaur that prowled over much of North Africa during the Late Cretaceous period.

FACTS

Name: *Carcharodontosaurus*
(car-CARE-oh-DON-tuh-SAW-rus)
Meaning: 'Shark-toothed lizard'
Classification: Theropod
Size: 10.5–13 m long
Weight: 7 tons
Diet: Meat (anything it fancied!)
Found: North Africa
When: Late Cretaceous, 97–90 million years ago

CARCHARODONTOSAURUS

Fossilized remains of *Carcharodontosaurus* (car-CARE-oh-DON-tuh-SAW-rus) have been found throughout North Africa, including teeth from Algeria, Tunisia, Sudan and Niger; cranial fragments and parts of a skeleton from Egypt; and a relatively complete skull from Morocco. It was discovered in the 1920s and described by Ernst Stromer, who also named *Spinosaurus* (see page 22), and after whom *Paralititan stromeri* (see page 34), is named. Stromer named the new discovery '*Carcharodontosaurus*' because its triangular-shaped teeth resembled those of the Great White Shark (*Carcharodon carcharias*) and did not curve back, like the teeth of most theropods.

Carcharodontosaurus was huge – bigger than the largest known *Tyrannosaurus* (TIE-ran-oh-SAW-rus), and even bigger than the predatory *Giganotosaurus* (JIH-ga-NO-toe-SAW-rus) from Argentina – making it the unrivalled title-holder of 'the biggest meat-eating dinosaur of all time'. (There have been recent claims that *Spinosaurus* was even bigger, but this is not certain.)

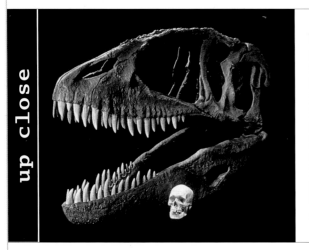

up close

When a human-sized skull is placed alongside a replica of the *Carcharodontosaurus* skull found in Morocco, it shows just how big the creature was. However, even though the dinosaur's skull is many times larger than a human's, our cranial capacity is 15 times bigger than that of this giant predatory creature, proving that big doesn't nessarily mean brainy!

RIGHT: Two predatory *Carcharodontosaurus* attack a juvenile plant-eating *Paralititan*, while the rest of the herd makes its getaway and pterosaurs circle overhead.

Although *Carcharodontosaurus* comes from North Africa, it is more closely related to *Giganotosaurus* than to the massive *Tyrannosaurus rex*, which comes from North America. This can be explained by the fact that the African and South American continents were joined for most of the Cretaceous period, enabling these large dinosaurs to roam over a vast landmass (see page 7).

In 1996, University of Chicago palaeontologist, Paul Sereno, excavated a skull of *Carcharodontosaurus* while he was working in the mountainous Kem Kem region of Morocco. This massive skull measured 1.6 m from the tip of its snout to the back of its head. Its upper jaw was lined with 14 blade-like teeth on either side (see photograph on opposite page). Each tooth measured about 15 cm in size and was a fierce cutting device with serrations (sharp, ragged cutting-edges, like those on the blade of a steak knife) that allowed it to 'cut' through the flesh of its unfortunate victims with ease. It was these distinctive triangular-shaped teeth that led to the dinosaur being named after the shark genus, *Carcharodon*.

T. rex, from North America, was almost as big as *Carcharodontosaurus*.

chapter six

The armoured sauropods

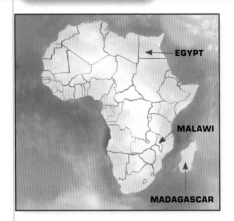

Africa, along with several other Gondwanan continents, was home to a group of long-necked armoured dinosaurs, called titanosaurs, which are distinctive for having had a protective armour of bone covering their body. This group includes *Malawisaurus* and *Karongasaurus* from Malawi, *Rapetosaurus* from Madagascar, and *Paralititan* from Egypt.

Paralititan holds the record for being the largest dinosaur ever found in Africa. It is also the third-largest dinosaur in the world, after the South American *Argentinosaurus*, and the recently discovered *Turiasaurus* from Spain.

up close

The preserved 'skin' of a titanosaur embryo (a baby dinosaur found still inside an egg). As the baby dinosaur grew, bone would develop inside the 'scales', which formed a rosette pattern. In contrast, the scales of adult dinosaurs could be quite large, as depicted below.

A 6 cm-long bony scute from an adult titanosaur.

TITANOSAURS

Titanosaurs were the last of the sauropods, or long-necked dinosaurs, to appear. They lived from the late Jurassic until the end of the Cretaceous. Their fossils are found in the southern continents that comprised Gondwana (see page 7). Titanosaurs are unique for having protective body armour, which consisted of bony scutes that developed within the dinosaur's skin. As with modern crocodilians (crocodiles and alligators), the titanosaur's bony armour varied in shape and size along the animal's body.

Crocodilians have a thick, scaly skin that forms a protective shield along the animal's body. Inside each of the scales is a thickened piece of bone, called a bony scute, that develops within the skin. In crocodiles, the scales, with their accompanying bony scutes, are larger and more roughly shaped along the top of the body, while along the sides and on the belly the scales and scutes are smaller and flatter, and sometimes rather poorly developed or even non-existent.

Close-up of a Nile crocodile, showing the 'scaly' skin. Bony scutes occur inside the scales, creating a protective 'armour'.

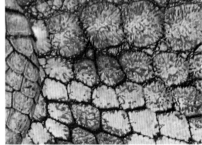

Along the sides of the crocodile's body, the scales and scutes are flatter than on the back.

RAPETOSAURUS

Even though the French geologist-palaeontologist Charles Depéret found 'armour' in the vicinity of a fossilized sauropod in Madagascar more than 100 years ago, it was uncertain whether the large, bony scutes actually belonged to the skeleton.

However, in 1995, the discovery, in northwestern Madagascar, of a *Rapetosaurus* skeleton alongside armour that clearly belonged to it, proved that these gigantic long-necked dinosaurs did indeed have thick bony scutes covering their bodies. This was also the first time that both an adult and a juvenile skull were found. The skulls showed very clearly that the nostrils were on top of the skull (not in front, as in a dog or cat). Although titanosaurs have been found on several of the Gondwanan continents (see page 7), the juvenile specimen of *Rapetosaurus* found in Madagascar is distinctive in that the skeleton was virtually complete, allowing almost every bone of its body to be identified and studied.

FACTS

Name: *Rapetosaurus*
 (Ra-PAY-to-SAW-rus)
Meaning: 'Mischievous giant
 lizard'
Classification: Sauropod
Size: 15 m long
Diet: Plants
Found: Madagascar
When: Late Cretaceous,
 70–65 million years ago

The plant-eating *Rapetosaurus* being attacked by a crocodile. At least seven different crocodiles have been recovered from the Late Cretaceous deposits in Madagascar, so it is quite possible that dinosaurs and crocodiles had some 'interactions'.

This skeletal reconstruction, based on a juvenile *Rapetosaurus* specimen, is about 75 per cent complete (only the bones shown in white are missing).

2 m

up close

Rapetosaurus had a long, flattish skull with nostrils on top of the snout. Its cylindrical, pencil-like teeth were efficient for raking off leaves but were not good for crushing and grinding plant matter. The teeth show high-angled wear facets which suggest tooth-against-tooth action.

MALAWISAURUS

Malawisaurus (mah-LAA-we-SAW-rus), the oldest titanosaur in the world, was found in the early 1990s in Malawi by palaeontologist Louis Jacobs and his colleagues from Southern Methodist University in Dallas, Texas.

The fossil comprises various parts of a skeleton, including part of the skull, several vertebrae, parts of the pelvis and some 'armour'. The armour consisted of both large and small scutes (scales), with the largest scute measuring 190 mm long and 95 mm wide. (Variations in the size of scutes have also been observed in the South American titanosaur, *Saltasaurus*.) *Malawisaurus* had a short, high skull that was held at the end of a long neck, a bulky body and a long tail.

ABOVE AND BELOW: *Malawisaurus* was excavated by a team from Southern Methodist University.

This mounted skeleton of *Malawisaurus* is on display at the Museum of Natural History in Dallas, Texas.

UNSOLVED

In addition to the remains of *Malawisaurus* and *Karongasaurus*, a differently structured tail vertebra was found during the excavations in Malawi, which suggests that a third titanosaur may have co-existed alongside them in the Early Cretaceous of Malawi.

ABOVE AND RIGHT: Excavating dinosaur bones can be a long, tedious process; here, local Malawians work alongside the team from Southern Methodist University to uncover dinosaur bones from the Early Cretaceous rocks of the Karonga district of northern Malawi. Both *Malawisaurus* and *Karongasaurus* were discovered in this area. *Karongasaurus* was described and named by Malawian palaeontologist Elizabeth Gomani (second from left in the photograph on the right).

KARONGASAURUS

In 2005, part of the lower jaw and some teeth of a titanosaur were found in in the Karonga district of Malawi and named *Karongasaurus* by Elizabeth Gomani, a Malawian palaeontologist.

Karongasaurus (Ka-RONGA-SAW-rus) lived at the same time as *Malawisaurus*. It had a long, low skull with cylindrical teeth that were present only in the front part of the jaw. Differences in the shape of the skull and teeth of titanosaurs from the Early Cretaceous of Malawi suggest that, although they lived in the same place, they ate different types of plant matter.

FACTS

Name: *Karongasaurus* (Ka-RONGA-SAW-rus)
Name refers to the Karonga district, in northern Malawi, where the fossil was found
Classification: Titanosaur
Size: Unknown
Diet: Plants
Found: Malawi
When: Early Cretaceous, 140–100 million years ago

UNSOLVED

Paralititan was not the only creature found in the fossil-bearing deposits of the Baharia Formation in Egypt. The remains of a large prehistoric fish (*Mawsonia*), a 10-metre-long crocodile, turtles, several lungfishes, and leaves and stems of a mangrove tree-fern were also recovered. These finds, together with the information recovered from the geological analysis, led the scientists to deduce that, in the mid-Cretaceous, about 95 million years ago, this part of Egypt was a lush mangrove-like environment near the seashore. It is possible that the large size of many of the animals found here is a response to the 'hot-house' conditions prevalent at that time.

American dinosaur expert Peter Dodson inspects the partially excavated humerus (forearm bone) of *Paralititan*.

PARALITITAN

The largest long-necked dinosaur discovered in Africa, and the third-largest in the world, is a titanosaur called *Paralititan*, which was recovered in 2001 from the Baharia Formation in Egypt by American palaeontologist, Josh Smith, and his team (see opposite). The remains consisted of a partial skeleton, including both forearm bones, several backbones (vertebrae), some ribs and shoulder bones.

This enormous dinosaur was some 30 m long and weighed about 90 tons (roughly the same length as eight African elephants lined up trunk to tail and the same weight as 16 large bull elephants!) This compares with *Argentinosaurus* (see page 28), the largest long-necked dinosaur in the world, which weighed in at 100 tons. The upper arm bone (humerus) of *Paralititan* measured 1.69 m (compared with that of *Argentinosaurus*, which is estimated to have been 1.81 m long).

Curiously, a 65 mm dinosaur tooth (possibly belonging to the carnivorous dinosaur *Carcharodontosaurus*, see page 28) was recovered among the skeletal remains of *Paralititan*. It doesn't take much imagination to guess at how a predatory dinosaur's tooth ended up alongside the skeleton of this gigantic herbivore (plant-eater)!

The second part of *Paralititan's* name (its species name) is '*stromeri*' in honour of the famous German palaeontologist-geologist Ernst Stromer who, in the early 1900s, led numerous field trips in North Africa and contributed enormously to the discovery of African dinosaurs. (See also page 22.)

TOP LEFT: Close-up of the heads of two of the long-necked sauropods that have been discovered in Africa: *Brachiosaurus* (left) from Tanzania and *Paralititan* (right) from Egypt.
CENTRE: This full reconstruction of a *Brachiosaurus* skeleton, alongside a human, shows its huge size.
BOTTOM LEFT: *Brachiosaurus'* footprint was large and almost circular. Huge, roundish sauropod footprints have been discovered in Zimbabwe's Zambezi Valley; some are almost a metre long and about 22 cm deep.

Besides being the largest animals ever to have lived on Earth, sauropods have the distinction of possessing the longest necks of any animal that ever lived, sometimes reaching about 9 m in length! What could these long necks have been used for? One suggestion is that they enabled them to reach high into tree-tops to browse. However, recent computer simulations suggest that many sauropods could not raise their necks much higher than their shoulders, but could stretch forward and very low, enabling them to feed on low-growing plants. Sauropods might also have used their necks to assert dominance (as giraffes do today), and it is possible that they may have reared onto their hind legs for short periods of time, as is depicted here in a fight between two long-necked dinosaurs.

Paralititan, an armoured sauropod from Egypt, is the largest dinosaur ever found in Africa. Here Josh Smith's joint team from the University of Pennsylvania and the Cairo Geological Museum is at work on the excavation site.

LEFT: At the site of the *Paralititan* excavation in Egypt, seven people were needed to lift the massive humerus out of the ground.

CENTRE: The full size of the bone, from the forearm of *Paralititan*, can be seen when measured against some of the team members, who are ready to start jacketing the underside of the bone in plaster of Paris (see page 9).

RIGHT: The excavated material was shipped to the Academy of Natural Sciences, Philadelphia, USA, where the proud team members were able to study the bones they had excavated.

chapter seven

The Mesozoic lawnmower

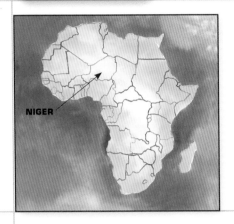

NIGER

The discovery of *Nigersaurus*, a small-bodied sauropod from the early Cretaceous rocks of the Gadoufaoua region of Niger, provided information about its unusual specializations for eating plants, as well as insight into how the sauropod dinosaurs changed over time.

FACTS

Name: *Nigersaurus*
(KNEE-jair-SAW-rus)
Meaning: Named after its
country of origin
Classification: Sauropod
Size: 15 m long; 3 m tall
Diet: Plants
Found: Niger
When: Early Cretaceous,
110 million years ago

UNSOLVED

The teeth of *Nigersaurus* have been fairly well studied by palaeontologists Paul Sereno and Jeff Wilson but, as yet, the scientists have been unable to determine exactly how the teeth batteries functioned to produce the rather unusual wear patterns visible on the teeth.

Because of its mouthful of teeth, *Nigersaurus* was nicknamed the 'Mesozoic lawnmower' by the popular American media.

NIGERSAURUS

Nigersaurus (KNEE-jair-SAW-rus) is one of the most common dinosaurs found in the fossil-bearing beds of the Gadoufaoua area of the Ténéré Desert in Niger. Other dinosaurs associated with these deposits are *Ouranosaurus* (a group-living, plant-eating dinosaur, see page 54), and the fish-eating *Suchomimus* (see page 24).

In 1999, University of Chicago palaeontologist Paul Sereno and his colleagues named and described *Nigersaurus* on the basis of a partial skeleton. This specimen is virtually complete with just a few bones missing from its feet, skull and the end of its tail. Studies of the *Nigersaurus* skeleton have shown that it is related to *Diplodocus*, a long-necked, plant-eating dinosaur discovered in North America and Tanzania (see page 45). Until this find, it was thought that the diplodocids were all extinct by the end of the Jurassic, but the discovery of *Nigersaurus* in the Cretaceous of Africa suggests that some survived. In addition to Sereno's find, *Nigersaurus* is represented by several other partial adult skeletons, isolated bones and teeth, as well as the tiny jaw of a baby *Nigersaurus*, which measures less than 8 cm in length.

Despite measuring about 15 m long, *Nigersaurus* was one of the smallest sauropods known. It was a plant-eater whose snout and jaws were specially adapted to allow it to process large quantities of plant matter. The lower jaws are unusual in that they are as broad as they are long, resulting in a wide snout, with teeth that extended across the front of the jaws.

When Paul Sereno, along with Jeff Wilson of the University of Michigan, studied the unusual teeth of *Nigersaurus,* they found that the lower jaw had 34 tooth positions, while the upper jaw had at least 20 tooth positions, and that within each of these 54 tooth positions there were as many as 10–12 columns of teeth. This means that about 600 needle-shaped teeth were present in *Nigersaurus'* jaws. The needle-shaped teeth (each about 4 mm in width) were closely packed together to form a 'battery' of teeth that erupted and wore down at the same time. *Nigersaurus* represents the first known occurence of tooth batteries among the sauropods. The teeth had gently curved, slender crowns that were oval in cross section. The tooth enamel was thicker on the outside than on the inside, towards the mouth cavity – possibly an adaptation for eating large quantities of plant matter.

OPPOSITE: *Nigersaurus* had a wide snout, with the teeth arranged across the front of the jaws. Palaeontologists think that the teeth were used for cropping vegetation rather than for chewing.

chapter eight

Ole wrinkle-face

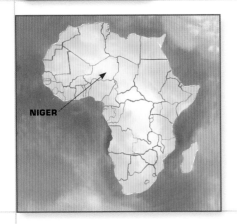

NIGER

Rugops is a large, meat-eating dinosaur discovered in the Sahara Desert. It belongs to a group of specialized predatory dinosaurs called abelisaurids (short-snouted theropods with small, pointy teeth) that are found exclusively on Gondwanan landmasses, and its discovery provides significant information about the radiation of abelisaurids. Since *Rugops* is one of the earliest abelisaurids discovered with a textured skull surface, it was named *Rugops primus*, which means 'first wrinkle-face'.

FACTS

Name: *Rugops* (ROO-gops)
Meaning: 'Wrinkle-face'
Classification: Theropod
Size: 7 m long
Diet: Meat
Found: Niger
When: Mid-Cretaceous, 95 million years old

UNSOLVED

Seven pairs of holes run along the animal's snout. No-one knows what their purpose was, but they may have been an ornamental feature, for display purposes only.

RUGOPS

Around 95 million years ago, what is now the vast expanse of the Sahara Desert was an area of wide rivers and lush vegetation that teemed with dinosaurs and other animals that are now extinct. In 2004, American palaeontologist Paul Sereno discovered *Rugops* (ROO-gops), a large, meat-eating dinosaur that once lived in the Ténéré region of Niger.

Rugops is known from a fairly complete skull, which shows that it had a short snout and small teeth. Because of the rather small, delicate-looking teeth and the overall shape of the skull, it is likely that *Rugops* scavenged for food instead of hunting down its prey.

The skull is unusual in that it is riddled with deep grooves that give the creature its name, 'wrinkle face'. A tough outer layer of skin or scales probably covered the skull, while a network of arteries and veins beneath the skin (that were closely associated with the skull and its outer covering) made the 'wrinkle' impressions in the skull.

Rugops appears to be an abelisaurid dinosaur. It is related to *Majungasaurus*, the cannibal dinosaur from Madagascar (see page 52), *Carnotaurus* from South America, and other abelisaurids from India. The discoveries of *Rugops* and *Spinostropheus* (SPINE-oh-STROFE-ee-us), an even older abelisaurid from Niger, have given us interesting ideas about how continental drift may have affected the distribution of dinosaurs (see page 7). Prior to these discoveries, no abelisaurids were known from Africa, which led researchers to think that the continent must have split from Gondwana about 120 million years ago. However, the discovery of African abelisaurids suggests that Africa, Madagascar, India and South America only drifted apart some 100 million years ago; until then, dinosaurs were free to roam throughout the landmasses that made up Gondwana, which explains why the remains of similar types of dinosaurs are found in these continents today.

Out in the field, palaeontologist Paul Sereno concentrates as he patiently excavates part of *Rugops'* jaw.

A parade of some of Africa's predatory dinosaurs (top to bottom): *Rugops,* the 'wrinkle face' from Niger; the 'horned lizard', *Ceratosaurus* from Tanzania; the fish-eating *Masiakasaurus* from Madagascar, and the 'big dead lizard', otherwise known as *Syntarsus,* from southern Africa.

chapter nine

TANZANIA

The long-necked giants of Tendaguru

About 145–155 million years ago, the area now known as Tanzania was home to many different kinds of dinosaurs, including some of the largest animals that have ever lived. It is from here that the best of the Late Jurassic dinosaurs from Africa have been unearthed.

The long-necked, plant-eating dinosaurs, or sauropods, that were discovered at Tendaguru, a site in southeastern Tanzania, are remarkably similar to examples of Late Jurassic dinosaurs found in the Morrison Formation (a geological formation in the western USA that is a rich source of fossils); *Brachiosaurus* and *Diplodocus* are common to both Africa and North America (see pages 44 and 45).

However, a conspicuous difference between the two localities is the poor representation of large predatory dinosaurs at the Tendaguru site. Only a fragmented skeleton of *Elaphrosaurus*, a small, meat-eating dinosaur, plus some isolated remains, suggest that large meat-eaters, such as *Ceratosaurus* (see page 39), may have been present at the Tendaguru locality.

DIPLODOCIDS VERSUS BRACHIOSAURIDS

The sauropods discovered at Tendaguru are represented by diplodocids and brachiosaurids. Brachiosaurids are more heavily built than diplodocids and have fairly short tails (A). Although they are very similar looking, diplodocids have whip-like tails and flattish skulls, and their teeth are restricted to the front of their jaws (B, and see illustration opposite). An important distinguishing feature of the brachiosaurids is that their front legs are as long as, or longer than, their back legs.

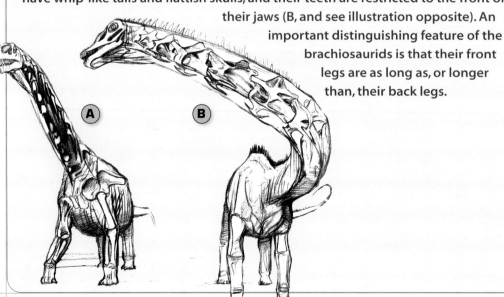

A   B

THE TENDAGURU 'DINOSAUR GRAVEYARD'

Between 1907 and 1913, German palaeontologist Wilhelm von Branca led a series of full-scale expeditions which resulted in more than 250 tons of fossil bones being excavated from Tendaguru, a remote locality in Tanzania, some 64 km from the coast. Tanganyika, as the country was then known, was a German colony at the time, so the fossils were taken to Berlin to be studied. During World War I, the German excavations stopped but, when Tanganyika became a British colony after the war, the excavations resumed and tons of new material was taken to the British Museum. During World War II, both the British Museum and Berlin's Natural History Museum, as well as several other sites in Germany that housed fossils from Tendaguru, were bombed, resulting in the loss of many of the original Tendaguru fossils.

DICRAEOSAURUS

Dicraeosaurus (die-KREE-oh-SAW-rus) is a well-known plant-eating diplodocid sauropod recovered from the Tendaguru deposits. The diplodocids are characterized by their extremely long necks and long, whip-like tails. It is likely that the diplodocids held their neck out when they walked, with the head almost horizontal, and the tail in a similar position at the rear to provide balance.

When *Dicraeosaurus* was discovered, palaeontologists realized that it had a rather short neck for a diplodocid, as well as unusual forked spines along its back and neck. In fact, it is these unusually shaped spines that gave this dinosaur its name, which means 'double-forked lizard'.

FACTS

Name: *Dicraeosaurus*
  (die-KREE-oh-SAW-rus)
Meaning: 'Double-forked lizard'
Classification: Sauropod
Size: 14 m long
Weight: 10 tons
Diet: Plants
Found: Tanzania
When: Late Jurassic,
  156–150 million years ago

UNSOLVED

The true function of the forked spines along *Dicraeosaurus*' back and neck is not known. It is possible the spines were ornamentations that made the docile plant-eating dinosaur appear fierce to its enemies.

up close

Dicraeosaurus had an array of spines along the neck and back, reaching almost all the way to the tip of its whip-like tail.

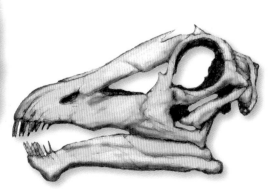

Skull of a diplodocid dinosaur. Notice how the teeth are limited to the front of the jaws.

The diplodocids may have used their long neck for asserting dominance (see page 35), while the whip-like tail could easily have been used for defence. They probably stretched out their neck and tail for balance when walking.

Brachiosaurus had a long neck, allowing it to browse on leaves growing high in the trees.

BRACHIOSAURUS (GIRAFFATITAN)

FACTS

Name: *Brachiosaurus*
(BRACK-ee-o-SAW-rus)
Also known as: Giraffatitan
Meaning: 'Arm lizard'
Classification: Sauropod
Size: 25 m long
Weight: 80 tons
Diet: Plants
Found: Tanzania
When: Late Jurassic,
155–145 million years ago

In 1914, German palaeontologist Werner Janensch found a skeleton at Tendaguru that was similar to *Brachiosaurus* (BRACK-ee-o-SAW-rus) found in the USA. The Tendaguru specimens were named *Brachiosaurus* but nowadays they are often referred to as *Giraffatitan* (Giraffe-a-TITAN), and there is some controversy as to whether they are related to *Brachiosaurus*.

The African *Brachiosaurus* (or *Giraffatitan*) is the tallest of the long-necked dinosaurs. It was named 'arm lizard' because its arms (forelimbs) were longer than the hind limbs. The skull has a distinctive, high crest, possibly to accommodate resonating (echoing) cavities that produced sounds used for communication (see 'Up close', opposite).

The *Brachiosaurus* remains collected from Tendaguru resulted in the mounting of a *Brachiosaurus* skeleton in Berlin's Natural History Museum (see opposite page).

OPPOSITE: Derek Ohland, of the Iziko South African Museum in Cape Town, standing next to a femur (thigh bone) that comes from a sauropod.

Close-up of *Brachiosaurus'* skull. Notice the large teeth, as well as the size of the head compared with the hands of the museum technician holding it.

up close

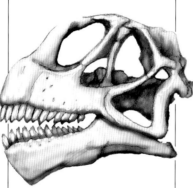

Brachiosaurus had a tall skull with large, spoon-shaped teeth that lined its jaws. The nares (nostrils) were located close to the top of the animal's head, and these large, hollow nasal cavities probably enabled the dinosaur to produce sounds.

This African *Brachiosaurus*, which is on display in the Natural History Museum in Berlin, Germany, is the tallest mounted skeleton in the world: it measures an enormous 13 m high and 23 m long. When the photograph was taken, the skeleton was being prepared for a new exhibition. Notice how small the people are compared with this gigantic sauropod, and how big it is compared with the other mounted dinosaurs alongside, *Dicraeosaurus* (on the left) and *Diplodocus* (on the right), which also come from the Tendaguru deposits.

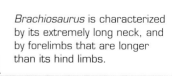

2 m

Brachiosaurus is characterized by its extremely long neck, and by forelimbs that are longer than its hind limbs.

chapter ten

The spiky African dinosaurs

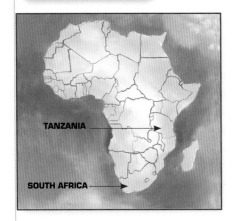

Plated dinosaurs, also known as stegosaurs, had a double row of large, bony plates, or spines, along their back, and most of them had spikes at the end of their tail. The exact function of the plates is not known, but they may have helped to keep the animal cool. The tail-spikes were probably used as weapons.

The best known plated dinosaur is *Stegosaurus*, which comes from North America, but several other plated dinosaurs have been found around the world. Two types of stegosaurs occurred in Africa: *Paranthodon* from South Africa and *Kentrosaurus* from Tanzania. In both species, the back plates are narrow and form spike-like projections along the top of the animal's body.

FACTS

Name: *Paranthodon*
  (Pah-RAN-tho-DON)
Meaning: 'Beside Anthodon'
Classification: Stegosaur
Size: Uncertain, but probably
  as big as Kentrosaurus
Diet: Plants
Found: South Africa
When: Early Cretaceous,
  130 million years ago

Cretaceous fossil-bearing rocks near Sundays River in the Eastern Cape.

up close

The remaining part of *Paranthodon's* upper jaw (± 16 cm), showing the leaf-shaped teeth.

PARANTHODON

Although *Paranthodon* (Pah-RAN-tho-DON) was the first stegosaur found in the world, and also the first dinosaur discovered in Africa, it was wrongly identified at the time. When fossilized bones were discovered near the Sundays River in the Eastern Cape in 1845 by Andrew Geddes Bain (the 'father' of South African geology) and William Atherstone, they thought the dinosaur was related to *Iguanodon*, a plant-eating dinosaur from Europe, and nicknamed it the 'Cape Iguanodon'. The excavated material included some very large, long bones that were described as the 'leg and hip bones of a reptile bigger than an ox'. All the material was sent to the British Museum, but no-one knows what happened to the collection of bones and all that remains is an upper jaw fragment (see 'Up close') containing the typical leaf-shaped teeth of stegosaurs, and two small skull fragments. This remaining skull material was misidentified, first as that of an early amphibian, then as that of an ankylosaur, until 1929 when it was correctly identified as the snout and upper jaw of a stegosaur and named *Paranthodon*.

In 1913, parts of leg bones, some vertebrae and several small fragments were found near to where the original *Paranthodon* was recovered. Unfortunately, these new fossils were later lost in a fire at the Albany Museum in Grahamstown.

Unlike *Stegosaurus* (STEG-oh-SAW-rus), *Paranthodon* did not have bony plates along its back. Instead, like its East African relative, *Kentrosaurus*, the plates were much narrower and formed large bony spikes or spines from the shoulders to about the middle of the tail. *Tuojiangosaurus*, a stegosaur discovered in China, was probably smaller than Stegosaurus but larger than *Kentrosaurus*; like its African relatives, the plates on *Tuojiangosaurus'* back were narrower and more pointed than those of *Stegosaurus*.

In 1995, the South African Postal Service issued a first-day cover to commemorate the 150th anniversary of the discovery of *Paranthodon*.

150ᵗʰ Anniversary

Paranthodon africanus (Broom)
First S.A. dinosaur discovery (1845-1995)

138/150

KENTROSAURUS

Kentrosaurus (KENT-ro-SAW-rus) was first discovered at Tendaguru in 1910 (see page 41). In addition to a double row of plates (spikes) along its back, *Kentrosaurus* had spikes that projected sideways from its shoulders, and a spiked 'club' at the end of its tail. These spikes would have made very effective weapons against attacking predators.

The remains of 40–50 *Kentrosaurus* individuals have been recovered from the Tendaguru area, suggesting they were fairly common there about 145 million years ago, and that they were social animals that lived in herds. In total, more than 1 200 stegosaur bones, including a one-metre-long spike from the tail region, have been unearthed from the Kindope quarry site at Tendaguru, as well as the remains of at least four stegosaurs whose bones were discovered all jumbled together. In addition to the stegosaur bones, the bones of other types of dinosaurs have been recovered from the area, including a sauropod femur (thigh bone) that measures 2.28 m in length – one of the largest dinosaur bones ever found.

The spikes on *Kentrosaurus*' back may have been used as defensive weapons against predators.

UNSOLVED

Stegosaurus may have used the large plates on its back to help regulate its body temperature, but the actual function of the narrow spines on the backs of some 'stegosaurs' is not known.

up close

Kentrosaurus bones held in the Earth Science collections at the Iziko South African Museum in Cape Town include arm bones (top: right and centre) and vertebrae, or spine bones (bottom).

10 cm

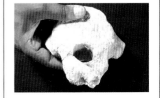

chapter eleven

The mythical monster

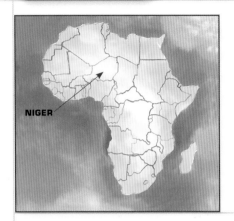

NIGER

By the time the first humans walked on Earth, about two million years ago, dinosaurs had already been extinct for some 63 million years. Early people probably came across dinosaur bones that were weathering out of sedimentary rocks, but it is unlikely that they knew these were the remains of creatures long extinct. However, evidence in the form of rock art suggests that the fossilized bones of these animals fascinated people from earlier times.

FACTS

Name: *Jobaria* (Jo-BAH-REE-ah)
Meaning: Named after the mythical creature 'Jobar'
Classification: Sauropod
Size: 18–21 m long
Diet: Plants
Found: Niger
When: Early Cretaceous, 135–130 million years ago

up close

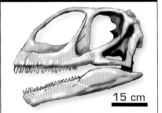

15 cm

Jobaria's broad teeth were adapted for nipping twigs off branches.

UNSOLVED

Skeletons of *Jobaria* reveal several primitive characteristics, such as its forelimbs being shorter than its hind limbs. It has a relatively short neck with only 12 cervical vertebrae, and about 20 unusually broad teeth in each of its upper and lower jaws. It is unclear why the group of sauropods to which *Jobaria* belongs retained these primitive features for tens of millions of years while sauropod groups that occurred elsewhere changed rapidly.

JOBARIA

In the Sahara Desert of central Niger, the local Tuareg people used to tell their children that the large bones that peeked out of the desert sands belonged to a mythical creature they called 'Jobar'. This changed in 1990, when a Tuareg chieftan showed some of the exposed fossil bones to visiting American palaeontologist Paul Sereno.

Sereno, from the University of Chicago, and his team excavated the remains of a 135-million-year-old sauropod (plant-eating dinosaur), and named it *Jobaria* (Jo-BAH-REE-ah) after the mythical Tuareg beast. Since then, several partial skeletons of *Jobaria*, as well as an isolated braincase from a teenage dinosaur, have been recovered, making *Jobaria* the most abundant large-bodied dinosaur found in Niger.

A *Jobaria* skeleton that was recovered from the Tiourarén Formation represents the most complete sauropod discovered in Africa, with about 95 per cent of the animal's bones having been preserved. (In geological terms, a formation is an assemblage of rocks of more or less the same age, that come from the same area. The rocks of the Tiourarén Formation date from the Early Cretaceous period, around 135–130 million years ago.)

Studies of *Jobaria* have shown that it is 'strikingly primitive'. It seems to represent an unknown lineage of broad-toothed sauropods that diverged (some 30–40 million years earlier) from all other Cretaceous sauropods such as diplodocids and brachiosaurids.

A cast of the *Jobaria* skeleton found in Niger being prepared for exhibition at the Iziko South African Museum in Cape Town. Although *Jobaria* was not as enormous as some sauropods, its size is evident when judged against the men standing alongside it.

DINOSAURS AND MYTHS

One of the earliest reports of what are probably dinosaur bones comes from Chang Qu, an ancient Chinese scholar who, in 300 BC, wrote about 'dragon bones' that were found in Sichuan province. Dragons are only mythological (imaginary) creatures, so it is possible that the bones he described came from dinosaurs, which have been found in that area.

In North America, the earliest depictions of dinosaurs occur in rock engravings (called petroglyphs) made by the Fremont people, who lived between AD 400 and 1500 in eastern Utah and north-western Colorado in the USA. At the Grand Staircase-Escalante National Monument in Utah, several petroglyph panels have been discovered that depict three-toed footprints and are probably based on Lower Jurassic fossil trackways that occur in the area.

In central Africa, the Congolese people believe in the legend of Mokele-Mbembe, a creature that lives in the Likouala Swamp and is said to resemble a sauropod. However, unlike 'Jobar', no dinosaur bones have been recovered from this area and the reported 'encounters' with Mokele-Mbembe are suspect.

Jobaria had a large claw on each front foot, and smaller claws on its back feet. Unlike other Sauropods of its time, *Jobaria* retained many primitive features, such as broad teeth in its jaws, and a relatively short neck and tail.

AFROVENATOR, THE HUNTER

At Fako, a fossil site in Niger, two sauropod skeletons were found, one on top of the other. The larger one, with a body length of about 18 m, was indentified as *Jobaria*. The two specimens had clearly been scavenged upon before being covered by sediment. Associated with the skeletons were the remains of three predatory dinosaurs: two small-bodied dinosaurs, and *Afrovenator* (Af-ro-veh-NAY-tur), the most complete theropod (meat-eating) dinosaur known from Africa – hence its common name 'hunter from Africa'.

Afrovenator is unusual in that it does not have the skull crests and rough, pitted surface texture (rugosities) seen in other theropod fossils (see page 38). But, like a good predatory dinosaur, *Afrovenator* has vicious sickle-shaped claws on its three-fingered hands, and large 5 cm-long, blade-like teeth in its jaws – both of which would have come in handy when attacking and killing its prey.

FACTS

Name: *Afrovenator*
   (Af-ro-veh-NAY-tur)
Meaning: 'Hunter from Africa'
Classification: Theropod
Size: 9 m in length
Diet: Meat
Found: Niger
When: Early Cretaceous,
   135–130 million years ago

Despite being much smaller than *Jobaria*, a pack of *Afrovenator* individuals could easily have attacked and brought down the plant-eating *Jobaria* to make a meal out of it. Perhaps the skeletons discovered at Fako were predator and prey that fell victim to some unknown catastrophe that killed them both.

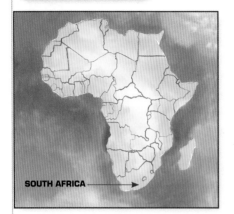

chapter twelve

SOUTH AFRICA

The only Xhosa-named dinosaur

The first dinosaur discovered in Africa, *Paranthodon*, was found in the Eastern Cape in 1845. Despite many dinosaur discoveries on the continent since then, it was to be another 155 years before a dinosaur was named in an indigenous southern African language. *Nqwebasaurus* is the name given to a small meat-eating dinosaur found in Nqweba, the Xhosa name for the Kirkwood region of the Eastern Cape.

FACTS

Name: *Nqwebasaurus*
   (n-KWE-bah-SAW-rus)
Meaning: 'Lizard from Nqweba'
Classification: Theropod
Height: 30 cm to hips
Size: 90 cm long
Diet: Meat
Found: Eastern Cape,
   South Africa
When: Early Cretaceous,
   135–130 million years ago

UNSOLVED

Besides *Nqwebasaurus*, other exquisitely preserved dinosaur bones were also found in the Kirkwood deposits. These had not been described at the time of going to print, but preliminary investigations suggest that they belong to a small ornithischian (see page 6).

NQWEBASAURUS

Over the years, many isolated fragments of bones have been recovered from the Early to Mid-Cretaceous rocks of the Kirkwood Formation. Between 1995 and 1997, palaeontologists from South Africa and the USA undertook a series of expeditions to the site of the Cretaceous deposits, which led to the discovery of even more dinosaur remains.

The most significant finding was made in 1996 by palaeontologists Callum Ross from the University of Chicago, and Billy De Klerk from Grahamstown's Albany Museum, who discovered a small meat-eating dinosaur, which they nicknamed 'Kirky', and which was later formally named *Nqwebasaurus thwazi* (n-KWE-bah-SAW-rus TWAH-zee). The first part of the name recognizes the place where it was found, while its species name, '*thwazi*', means 'fast runner'.

This was the first nearly complete, articulated dinosaur skeleton found in the Kirkwood Formation. Although only fragments of the skull survived, the rest of the beautifully preserved fossilized skeleton that was found enabled the specimen to be identified as a theropod dinosaur and, more specifically, a coelurosaur (a specialized group of theropod dinosaurs that are closely related to birds). Until this find, it was thought that coelurosaurs were rare on the Gondwanan continents (see page 7), and that they occurred only in the Late Cretaceous deposits of North Africa. The discovery of *Nqwebasaurus* challenged these ideas and showed that coelurosaurs were present in Gondwana during the Early Cretaceous, about 130 million years ago.

Measuring just 90 cm from its snout to tail-tip, *Nqwebasaurus* was a small, slightly built creature, as shown by these delicate bones, which come from its right foot.

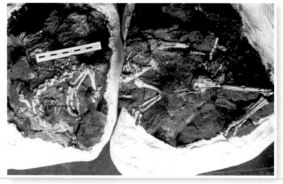

The excavated skeleton of *Nqwebasaurus*, protected by a plaster of Paris jacket, is on display in the Albany Museum, Grahamstown.

The reddish and grey mudstones of the Kirkwood Formation have yielded *Nqwebasaurus* and other dinosaur remains.

The author with geologist/palaeontologist Billy De Klerk, of the Albany Museum, at the site where the partial skeleton of *Nqwebasaurus* was found.

GASTROLITHS

Twelve small, roundish stones, called gastroliths, were found in the stomach region of the excavated skeleton of *Nqwebasaurus*. Gastroliths are thought to have helped animals digest the food they ate, and are fairly well known in the fossil record. Some modern animals, particularly birds and crocodiles, regularly use stones to help them digest their food. (See project on page 63.)

A microscopic section of *Nqwebasaurus'* femur (thigh bone) showing several growth rings, which indicate that the individual is a small-bodied adult, not a baby dinosaur.

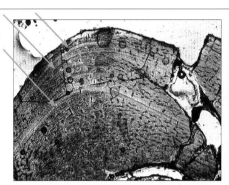

up close

Although the *Nqwebasaurus* fossil was relatively small in size, the presence of both fused and unfused bones suggests that it was not a very young individual. Evidence in the microstructure of the bones revealed that it had experienced at least three growth cycles (see page 15). However, the overall texture of the bone suggested that it was still growing and had not yet reached a mature body size.

Nqwebasaurus is thought to have been a coelurosaur, a specialized group of theropods that are closely related to birds.

chapter thirteen

The cannibal dinosaur

MADAGASCAR

A cannibal is an animal that eats the flesh of its own kind. Although many of the meat-eating mammals, reptiles and birds that we know of today show some cannibalistic behaviour, cannibalism seems to have been rare among dinosaurs. *Majungasaurus*, which comes from Madagascar, provides the first definitive evidence of cannibalism among dinosaurs.

MAJUNGASAURUS

FACTS

Name: *Majungasaurus*
(mah-JOONG-gah-SAW-rus)
Meaning: 'Lizard from Majunga'
Classification: Theropod
Size: 7–9 m long
Diet: Meat
Found: Madagascar
When: Late Cretaceous, 70 million years ago

In the summer of 2005, a team of palaeontologists from the USA and Madagascar, led by David Krause, unearthed the remains of several dinosaurs that were buried together some 70 million years ago near Majunga, a village in northern Madagascar. Careful study of the rocks, and the way the remains were preserved, suggested the dinosaurs had been buried at different stages over a long period of time. On the basis of all the evidence the researchers uncovered, they deduced that the animals had all died during periods of drought.

However, many of the fossilized bones discovered in three separate 'bone beds' had distinct bite marks on them. Suprisingly, most of the bitten bones seemed to belong to a predatory dinosaur called *Majungasaurus* (mah-JOONG-gah-SAW-rus). This suggested that one predatory dinosaur was dining on the carcasses of another – but which predatory dinosaur was the culprit? After careful study of the jaws and teeth of possible candidates, the palaeontologists concluded that the grooves and gnaw-marks on the bones could only have been caused by the blade-like serrated teeth of *Majungasaurus* itself, which strongly suggests that it was eating its own kind.

Majungasaurus's species name is 'atopus' (AT-o-pus), which means 'out of place'. When part of a skull with a thickened 'dome' was first found, it was misidentified as a *Pachycephalosaur* (a dinosaur with a solid, thickened dome of bone on the top of its skull). However, the later discovery of a well preserved skull showed that the misidentified 'dome' was actually part of a distinctive 'horn' on *Majungasaurus'* forehead – which explains its species name 'out of place'. The horn, together with other features of its skull, show that *Majungasaurus* was related to the abelisaurids (see page 38), such as *Carnotaurus* from South America, and others from India, adding to the evidence that, 70 million years ago, the landmasses of South America, Africa, Madagascar, the Indian subcontinent and Antarctica were all joined (see page 7).

up close

A reconstruction of *Majungasaurus'* skull, based on the remains found at Majunga. The external surface of the bone is roughly pitted, the top of the skull has thick ornamentations on it, and a low horn is present. From the tip of the snout to the back of the skull it measures 57 cm.
  The original skull was extremely well preserved, making it one of the most complete dinosaur skulls known. The whole skull was disarticulated, which means that all the individual bones were separate and, because the bones were not distorted, they made the skull very easy to study and to reconstruct.

Tooth marks on this *Majungasaurus'* bone fragment match the size and spacing of its teeth, suggesting that this dinosaur was a cannibal and dined on its own kind.

Did dinos eat their own kind?
There have been suggestions that tyrannosaurs may have chewed on the bones of their own relatives, but the evidence presented is not conclusive.

Many years ago, at the Ghost Ranch quarry in New Mexico, in the USA, where the remains of several *Coelophysis* specimens were recovered, scientists found the remains of a young *Coelophysis* closely associated with the remains of an adult individual. This seemed to suggest cannibalism among *Coelophysis*, but it could not be substantiated.

Although evidence suggests that *Majungasaurus* ate its own kind, scientists are not sure whether the killing was deliberate or whether it may simply have scavenged on the body of a dead 'relative'.

There is evidence that *Majungasaurus* fed on the sauropod *Rapetosaurus* (as depicted here), but there is also evidence that *Majungasaurus* practised cannibalism, that is, fed on its own kind.

Sociable dinosaurs

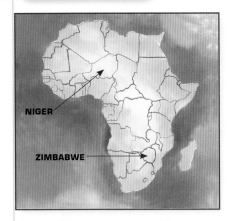

NIGER

ZIMBABWE

FACTS

Name: *Ouranosaurus*
  (oo-RAHN-oh-SAW-rus)
Meaning: 'Brave monitor
  lizard'
Classification: Ornithischian
Size: 7 m long
Diet: Plants
Found: Niger
When: Early Cretaceous,
  110 million years ago

Today, large herds of herbivorous mammals, such as zebra and wildebeest, can be seen on Africa's plains. These highly social animals gather at watering holes to drink, and they tend to herd together during the mating season or before setting off on seasonal migrations to new feeding grounds. In contrast, predatory mammals often live solitary lives, although some, such as lions and wild dogs, form small packs, and hunt and care for their young together.

Dinosaur fossils provide good evidence that many herbivorous dinosaurs lived in large herds, while several predatory dinosaurs lived and hunted in packs. *Ouranosaurus*, a plant-eating dinosaur, typically moved about in large herds, while *Syntarsus* is an example of a predatory dinosaur that teamed up with others of its kind to form a small, but efficient, hunting pack.

OURANOSAURUS

In the 1960s, French palaeontologists made several expeditions to the southern Sahara. In the Ténéré Desert in Niger, Philippe Taquet and his team found six *Ouranosaurus* skeletons together, proof that they must have died in a group.

Ouranosaurus (oo-RAHN-oh-SAW-rus) is distinguished by a 'sail' or ridge along its back. Up to 50 cm high, the ridge was formed by extensions of the backbone and ran from the creature's shoulders to halfway down its tail. *Ouranosaurus* has been referred to as the 'African iguanodontian', because of the many similarities it shows to *Iguanodon* (Ih-GWANO-oh-don), which was one of the first dinosaurs to be named. However, it is now thought that *Ouranosaurus* is more closely related to the hadrosaurs, or 'duck-billed dinosaurs', than to the iguanodontians. *Ouranosaurus* had an unusually flat head, with a raised bony brow above the eyes and a sloping snout leading to a wide, bill-like mouth. No front teeth were present but, along the sides of the jaws, *Ouranosaurus* had a large battery of teeth.

Ouranosaurus were plant-eaters with sturdy back legs that were longer than their front legs. Its forelimbs had a distinctive thumb with a huge, sharp thumb-spike, which could have been a weapon or used for grasping trees. When a fossilized thumb-spike of *Iguanodon* was first discovered, it was thought to be a horn on the animal's head. However, when a partial skeleton was found, it clearly showed that the spike was located on the thumb, and not on the creature's head.

up close

A fossilized *Ouranosaurus* 'sail': the sail-like feature was made up of bony extensions of the vertebrae (backbones). Around the middle of the back, these extensions were about 50 cm high (that is, just 10 cm short of two long rulers placed end to end).

Social dinosaurs living in herds would likely have interacted with each other, as these two *Ouranosaurus* individuals are doing. Touching may have been used to reinforce kinship bonds or perhaps for greeting herd members.

SYNTARSUS

The best African example of a predatory pack-living dinosaur has been called by various names: *Syntarsus*, *Coelophysis* and *Megapnosaurus*. It belonged to the theropods, a diverse group of predatory (meat-eating) dinosaurs.

In 1969, in the fine-grained sandstone at Mana Pools National Park in the Zambezi Valley, local palaeontologist Mike Raath found skeletons of about 30 individuals of a medium-sized, meat-eating dinosaur, which he named *Syntarsus*. The bones were jumbled together, suggesting the animals may have died in a flood. Anatomical studies of the remains showed that the pack was made up of individuals of different sizes – juveniles, teenagers and adults. On the basis of distinctive features found in the adult thigh bones, Raath suggested they were male and female dinosaurs.

There is confusion over *Syntarsus'* name: for a while it was considered to be the same genus as the North American *Coelophysis*, but it is now regarded as belonging to a different genus. However, it turns out that '*Syntarsus*' cannot be used for a dinosaur as, more than 100 years ago, this name was allocated to a beetle. As a result, a new name, *Megapnosaurus*, which means 'big dead lizard', has been proposed for *Syntarsus*.

FACTS

Name: *Syntarsus* or *Megapnosaurus*
Meaning: 'Fused ankle' or 'Big dead lizard'
Classification: Theropod
Size: 3 m long
Weight: 20 kg
Diet: Meat
Found: Zimbabwe
When: Early Jurassic, 190 million years ago

DINOSAUR GRAVEYARDS

The distribution of skeletal remains and dinosaur tracks strongly suggests that many types of dinosaur lived in groups: some fossil localities are even referred to as 'dinosaur graveyards' because of the high concentration of skeletal remains found in a small area. The Tendaguru dinosaur deposits in Tanzania, and Dinosaur Provincial Park in Canada, are examples of such places.

At some sites, large numbers of individuals of particular types of dinosaur are found together, for example, *Kentrosaurus* from the Tendaguru locality (see page 40). These rich fossil deposits suggest that, in the Mesozoic, many herbivores, such as the ceratopsians (frilled and horned dinosaurs), lived in large herds. Many finds of dinosaur herds suggest that they died in catastrophic events such as a flood, drought or sudden volcanic activity. In contrast to the more peaceful herbivores, evidence suggests that meat-eating dinosaurs tended to exhibit pack behaviour, coming together mainly to hunt, mate and rear their young. This includes large predators, such as *Tyrannosaurus rex*, as well as small to medium-sized ones, like *Syntarsus*.

Two *Syntarsus* (*Megapnosaurus*) individuals engage in a tug-of-war over a tasty meal, while in the foreground, a small furry mammal and several tiny creatures scurry off hurriedly. Other members of the pack can be seen in the background.

chapter fifteen

The flying dinosaurs

MADAGASCAR

The history of birds extends back into the fossil record about 150 million years, to a time when dinosaurs were the dominant land animals. Scientists generally agree that birds are descendants of dinosaurs, and so we can quite accurately refer to birds as dinosaurs! Although early birds spread throughout the world, the fossilized birds discovered in Madagascar are the only Mesozoic birds known from Africa. Two of these, *Vorona* and *Rahonavis*, provide important clues about the Late Cretaceous period birds of the region (see pages 60 and 61).

FACTS

Name: *Archaeopteryx*
(ARE-kee-OP-tair-icks)
Meaning: 'Ancient wing'
Classification: Aves (Bird)
Size: 60 cm
Diet: Meat
Found: Germany
When: Late Jurassic,
150 million years ago

ARCHAEOPTERYX – THE 'FIRST BIRD'

The first bird fossil, a single feather, was discovered in 1860, in Solnhofen in Germany. A year later, when the first skeleton of a feathered creature was discovered in the same location, it caused a sensation, as it had features that were both reptile-like (teeth in its beak and a long, bony tail) and bird-like (feathers and long arms). It was named *Archaeopteryx* (ARE-kee-OP-tair-icks), and is the earliest known bird. Today, eight specimens of *Archaeopteryx* are known, all from the same region and all with beautifully preserved feather impressions. Many fossilized birds dating from the Mesozoic Era (see page 6) have been discovered around the world, but they are rare on the African continent.

In the 1970s, small three-toed tracks found in Early Jurassic beds in South Africa were thought to have been made by early birds, but recent studies of these tracks suggest they were made by small non-avian dinosaurs, rather than birds. Early bird tracks have been described from the Late Cretaceous beds of Morocco but, except for these tracks, and one possible bird vertebra from Morocco's Kem-Kem region, no other fossils of Mesozoic birds are known from the mainland of Africa.

However, in 1995, on a joint expedition in Madagascar, US palaeontologist David Krause and his team discovered a rich Cretaceous fossil locality in the Majunga Basin. Here, American and Madagascan scientists discovered three species of bird: *Rahonavis*, *Vorona* and the remains of another basal bird, as well as fossils of theropods such as the cannibal *Majungasaurus* (see page 52) and the fish-eating *Masiakasaurus* (page 25).

up close

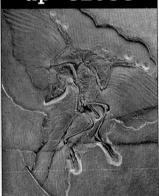

One of the finest fossil specimens of *Archaeopteryx*. The impressions of feathers on the wings, body and tail are all clearly visible, as are its long bony tail and long neck. This prized specimen, found in Germany in 1877, is now in the Natural History Museum in Berlin, Germany.

BIRD BONES UNDER THE MICROSCOPE

Modern birds grow very rapidly, reaching their adult body size within a few weeks, and the structure of their bones reflects this fast growth rate. Microscopic studies of the bones of *Rahonavis* and *Vorona* show that, unlike modern birds, they grew rapidly to a certain stage, and thereafter grew in alternating slow and fast cycles, with distinct pauses in between. These cycles of slow and fast growth formed 'rings' in the bone, which suggest that early birds grew more slowly than modern birds, and took several years to reach a mature body size. (See also page 15.)

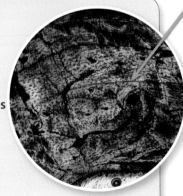

Bone microstructure of *Vorona* reveals ring-like growth cycles, interspersed with periods when no growth took place (arrowed).

Archaeopteryx, the 'first bird', showed intermediate features between theropod dinosaurs and birds: clawed 'fingers' along the front edges of its wings, a long bony tail covered in feathers, and teeth in its jaws.

UNSOLVED

Phylogenetic studies have shown that *Rahonavis* and *Vorona* are not directly related to the indigenous birds found in Madagascar today. It is still uncertain whether these ancestors of modern birds were present on the island before it split from Africa in the Late Cretaceous or whether they flew in afterwards.

VORONA

Vorona (vor-OON-ah) represents the first Cretaceous bird described from Africa. Its remains were found near the village of Berivotra in northwestern Madagascar. Even though the find consisted of only some leg bones, American palaeontologist Cathy Forster and her collaborators were able to ascertain how *Vorona* was related to other Mesozoic birds and that these were indirectly related to modern birds found in Madagascar today. Detailed studies of the bones of *Rahonavis* and *Vorona* showed that they both grew much slower when compared with modern birds.

up close

0.5 cm

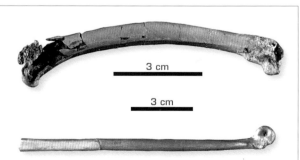

3 cm

3 cm

Vorona bones: On the left is a view into the hollow shaft of a tibiotarsus (a long leg bone in birds, formed by the fusion of the ankle and tibia, or shin bone). Bird bones have a hollow central cavity and thin walls to make them lightweight, an essential adaptation for creatures that fly. On the right are a femur or thigh bone (top), and an almost complete tibiotarsus (bottom).

The predatory *Rahonavis* flying alongside the titanosaur *Rapetosaurus*, which acts as a handy landing site for several other birds. The sickle-shaped claw on *Rahonavis'* second toe is clearly visible.

RAHONAVIS

When Cathy Forster, a palaeontologist from George Washington University in the USA, and her colleagues studied the skeletal remains (some limbs, part of the hip and shoulder bones, and several vertebrae) of *Rahonavis* (Ra-HOON-AVE-iss), they found that this Late Cretaceous bird was closely related to *Archaeopteryx*, the earliest known bird (see page 58).

Rahonavis, which was about the size of a modern-day hawk, had many features in its skeleton that are similar to those of modern birds – such as attachment areas for flight feathers on the bones of its forearms. It also had some primitive features, such as a long tail, that were similar to those of earlier dinosaurs. However, perhaps *Rahonavis'* most spectacular feature was a large, retractable, sickle-shaped claw on its second toe. This would have been used for slashing at enemies or for attacking prey.

Rahonavis' claw is very similar to the claws found on other top dinosaurian predators, such as *Deinonychus*, a fast-moving killer whose name means 'terrible claw'.

up close

A set of well-preserved *Rahonavis* foot bones. The large, sickle-shaped claw on the second toe was used in self-defence and also as a very effective weapon.

1 cm

FACTS

Name: *Rahonavis*
  (Ra-HOON-AVE-iss)
Meaning: 'Bird menace from
  the clouds'
Classification: Aves (Bird)
Size: 30–50 cm
Diet: Meat
Found: Madagascar
When: Late Cretaceous,
  83–70 million years ago

chapter sixteen

Five fun projects

MAKE A CAST OF A 'FOSSIL'

You will need:
Plaster of Paris
Modelling clay or Plasticine™
'Fossil' (e.g. a leaf, feather, bone or seashell)
Coloured paints

1 Roll out a piece of clay to be slightly larger than your 'fossil' and about 2 cm thick. Use some more clay to build a wall about 2 cm high around the flat piece of clay to make a well. Press your 'fossil' firmly into the clay, then remove it (an impression of it will be left in the clay).

2 Mix some plaster of Paris with water to make a sloppy mixture (above); pour the mixture into the well and leave it to set (below).

3 Once the plaster of Paris is hard, carefully remove the clay from around it. You will be left with a cast of the 'fossil', which you can paint.

MAKE A DINOSAUR MODEL

You will need:
Potters' clay or modelling clay and coloured paints

1 First decide what type of dinosaur you want to make, for example, a long-necked sauropod, like *Brachiosaurus* (page 44) or a predatory dinosaur like *Majungasaurus* (page 52).

2 Divide the clay into eight pieces, and shape them into two legs, two arms, a body, a tail, a neck and a head. The length of the hind legs and forelegs (arms) will depend on the type of dinosaur you're modelling.

3 Press the pieces of clay together to form a model of your dinosaur. You can add skin texture such as scales or feathers.

4 Potters' clay can be fired in a kiln, and modelling clay can be put into the oven to harden (this may require an adult's help). Some types of clay can be dried in the sun.

5 Once the clay has dried, the dinosaur can be painted. Use the illustrations in this book to help you choose your colours.

EXAMINE TRACKS MADE IN SAND

When you find tracks at the beach or in a sandy clearing, try to work out what sort of animal made the tracks. Some things to consider are:

- Did it walk on two feet or on four?
- Was it going in a particular direction?
- Was it walking alone or in a group?
- Can you determine anything about the size of the animal or person, as well as their companions?
- If the tracks were made by a person, was he/she walking with another person, or with a dog?
- Was the person barefoot or wearing shoes?
- Was the person walking or running?

- Is the depth of the footprints the same or does it vary? (In sand, the depth of the impression will depend on how wet the sand was when the tracks were made; wetter sand creates deeper impressions.)

- If possible, take photographs or draw the tracks and record the information. When you get home, write up your findings.

DINOSAUR QUIZ

Search the pages of this book to find the answers to these questions. See page 64 for the correct answers.

1 Name two stegosaurs found in Africa. (2 points)

2 What is the biggest meat-eating (predatory) dinosaur called? (1 point)

3 What is the name of the earliest known bird? (1 point)

4 Name two Mesozoic birds found in Africa. (2 points)

5 Where is *Masiakasaurus* found? (1 point)

6 Name three fish-eating dinosaurs found in Africa. (3 points)

7 What is *Sarcosuchus*? (1 point)

8 What is the name of South Africa's Xhosa-named dinosaur? (1 point)

9 Which dinosaur is considered to be the earliest sauropod (long-necked dinosaur)? (1 point)

10 What does the word 'dinosaur' mean? (1 point)

11 Which dinosaur is known as the 'Mesozoic lawnmower'? (1 point)

12 In which country was *Jobaria* found? (1 point)

Score: 16/16 – Excellent 10/16 – Good
Below 10 – Bad luck; read some more and try again.

TEST THE EFFECTIVENESS OF STOMACH STONES (GASTROLITHS)

Palaeontologists often find small, polished, rounded stones in the abdominal area of dinosaurs. This is especially common among plant-eating dinosaurs (e.g. *Massospondylus*, page 12), but is also known among meat-eating forms (e.g. *Nqwebasaurus*, page 50). Stomach stones are common in modern animals and have been found in the digestive systems of ostriches, crocodiles and seals. They appear to help animals digest their food and, in aquatic animals, may act as ballast (weight to help them overcome buoyancy). We can assume that the presence of gastroliths in the digestive tracts of dinosaurs probably functioned to aid digestion.

You will need:
Two empty glass or plastic jars with lids that seal
Small, smooth stones to act as the gastroliths
Some tough plant leaves from your garden
Tap water

1 Divide the leaves into two equal piles. Place one batch of leaves into each empty jar. Add the small stones to one jar (leave the other without any stones).

2 Half-fill each jar with water. Close the jars and shake each jar for about two minutes.

3 Compare the contents of each jar (i.e. which jar has more mashed-up leaves) and write up your findings.

Index

AUTHOR'S ACKNOWLEDGEMENTS

I have had such fun working on this book, and I hope that it will delight you to read about Africa's exceptional dinosaurs. It has been an absolute pleasure to work with Luis Rey, who skillfully breathes life into dinosaurs with his stunning artwork. I am indebted to my family and friends for inspiring me to write a book dedicated to African dinosaurs, and I am especially grateful to Tony Fairall for ensuring that this did finally happen. Peter Dodson is warmly thanked for having checked the accuracy of the writing and for always being just an email away.

I am most appreciative to the following people who have been so generous with images and who so willingly shared information or assisted me in some way or the other: Luis Chiappe, Kristi Currey-Rogers, Cristiano dal Sasso, Billy de Klerk, Peter Dodson, Atakan Ergeneci, Tony Fiorillo, Jørn Hurum, Louis Jacobs, Sheena Kaal, Patti Kane-Vanni, Lucy Kemp, David Krause, Thomas Lehmann, Derek Ohland, Andrea Plos, Robert Reiz, Hamish Robertson, Paul Sereno, Roger Smith, Philippe Taquet, Kerwin van Willingh and Adam Yates. The following institutions permitted access to their dinosaur collections: Museum für Naturkunde, Berlin; Bernard Price Institute for Palaeontological Research, University of the Witwatersrand; and the Iziko South African Museum in Cape Town. Pippa Parker, Janice Evans, Louise Topping and Gill Gordon of Struik are warmly thanked for their enthusiastic support.

I am most grateful to my husband, Yunus Turan, for always supporting and encouraging my many ventures. Lastly, I am deeply thankful to my son, Evren, for his careful reading and insightful comments that have no doubt improved the clarity of this book for his peers. Finally, thanks to you, dear reader, for your interest in African dinosaurs; this book was written with you in mind!

QUIZ ANSWERS (from page 63) 1. *Paranthodon* (page 46), *Kentrosaurus* (page 47); 2. *Carcharodontosaurus* (page 28); 3. *Archaeopteryx* (page 58); 4. *Rahonavis* and *Vorona* (pages 60–61); 5. Madagascar (page 25); 6. *Spinosaurus* (page 22), *Suchomimus* (page 24), *Masiakasaurus* (page 25); 7. A flesh-eating crocodile OR a crocodilian (page 24); 8. *Nqwebasaurus* (page 50); 9. *Antetonitris* (page 20); 10. Terrible lizard (page 5); 11. *Nigersaurus* (page 36); 12. Niger (page 48).